12-HOUR SLOW COOKER RECIPES

Cooking slow while you're on the go

Printed in the United States of America
by G&R Publishing Co.

Distributed By:

507 Industrial Street
Waverly, IA 50677

ISBN-13: 978-1-56383-222-2
ISBN-10: 1-56383-222-4
Item #7014

Table of Contents

When Slow Isn't Slow Enough...

The idea behind the 12-Hour Slow Cooker Cookbook is that, sometimes, slow cooker recipes just aren't slow enough. Think about it... as a typical American working person, your day starts early. After your morning and afternoon commutes, the full work day and some necessary errands, it is often 10 or 11 hours before you even return home in the evening. Wouldn't it be nice to walk into the house after your exhausting day to discover that dinner has been cooking while you were gone... and all you have to do is dish it up for dinner?!?!

The recipes within this book have been professionally tested, allowing you to spend more time relaxing or enjoying moments with family and friends and less time fumbling around in the kitchen. Each recipe lists the approximate amount of prep time needed to assemble the ingredients, which is often only 10 to 15 minutes, and approximate serving size for the meal. In most cases, you simply need to place the ingredients in your slow cooker, turn it on and continue with your daily activities.

The 12-hour slow cooker recipes are divided into categories for soups and stews, beef, chicken, pork and miscellaneous recipes, such as Red Beans & Rice, Fresh Herbed Turkey and Southwestern Enchiladas. There is also a section for Breakfast recipes intended to cook throughout the night, allowing you to wake-up to a piping hot breakfast that you won't have to lift a finger to prepare – it's almost too good to be true! But it is true, and we are certain this cookbook will become a staple in your kitchen and shed new light on cooking slow. Enjoy!

BEEF

Basic Pot Roast

Prep Time: 10 minutes

Cook Time: 10-12 hours

Servings: 6-8

Ingredients:

3 medium potatoes

3 medium carrots

2 medium onions

3 stalks celery with leaves

1 tsp. salt

¼ tsp. pepper

1 (3 to 4 lb.) pot or rump roast

1 bay leaf

3 beef bouillon cubes

½ C. water

1 T. Worcestershire sauce

Peel the potatoes, carrots and onions. Cut the potatoes in half and cut the carrots and onions into quarters. Slice the celery stalks with leaves into 2" pieces. Place half of the vegetables across bottom of slow cooker.

Rub salt and pepper completely over roast and place roast in slow cooker over vegetables. Place remaining vegetables around roast and add bay leaf and bouillon cubes. Pour water and Worcestershire sauce over ingredients.

Cover and cook on low setting for 10 to 12 hours. To serve, remove roast and vegetables to a serving platter. Let roast cool just slightly before slicing.

Beef Burgundy

Prep Time: 10 minutes

Cook Time: 10-12 hours

Servings: 4

Ingredients:

2 lbs. boneless beef chuck

1 (8 oz.) pkg. whole
mushrooms

1 tsp. salt

¼ tsp. pepper

1½ tsp. paprika

1 (12 oz.) pkg. frozen pearl
onions

1 large bell pepper, chopped

¾ C. dry red wine

1 bay leaf

2 beef bouillon cubes

Trim excess fat from beef chuck and cut into 1" to 2" cubes. Wash mushrooms and cut into quarters.

In a small bowl, combine salt, pepper and paprika. Mix well and sprinkle over beef cubes, until well coated. Place quartered mushrooms, pearl onions and chopped bell pepper across bottom of slow cooker. Add seasoned beef cubes, dry red wine, bay leaf and beef bouillon cubes.

Cover and cook on low setting for 10 to 12 hours. To serve, remove meat and vegetables to a serving platter. Spoon liquid from slow cooker over all.

Spiced Pepper Steak

Prep Time: 10-15 minutes

Cook Time: 10-12 hours

Servings: 6

Ingredients:

1 (2½ lb.) ½" thick beef round steak

¼ C. flour

½ tsp. salt

½ tsp. pepper

1 medium onion, chopped

1 clove garlic, minced

2 large green bell peppers, seeded

1 (16 oz.) can whole tomatoes in juice

1 T. beef bouillon granules

1 T. soy sauce

2 tsp. Worcestershire sauce

Prepared hot rice for serving

Cut round steak into strips. In a medium bowl, combine flour, salt and pepper. Place steak strips in flour mixture and toss until evenly coated. Place coated steak strips in slow cooker and add chopped onion and minced garlic. Cut green peppers into ½" strips and add half of the green pepper strips to slow cooker.

In a separate bowl, combine whole tomatoes in juice, beef bouillon, soy sauce and Worcestershire sauce. Mix well and pour mixture over ingredients in slow cooker.

Cover and cook on low setting for 10 to 12 hours. During last 1 hour of cooking time, add remaining half of the green pepper strips. To serve, divide prepared hot rice evenly onto serving plates. Spoon peppers, steak strips and sauce over rice on each plate.

4

Steak Roulade

Prep Time: 10-15 minutes

Cook Time: 10-12 hours

Servings: 2-4

Ingredients:

2 (1½ lb. each) thin round steaks

2 tsp. salt

2 tsp. pepper

¾ C. finely chopped onions

¼ C. finely chopped celery

¾ C. chopped bacon

¼ C. water

2 beef bouillon cubes

Trim excess fat from round steaks and season with salt and pepper. Spread an even amount of chopped onions, chopped celery and chopped bacon over each steak. Roll steaks from short end and use kitchen string to tie steak in several places, enclosing the onions, celery and bacon.

Place steaks in slow cooker and add water and beef bouillon cubes. Cover and cook on low setting for 10 to 12 hours.

Swiss Steak

Prep Time: 10-15 minutes

Cook Time: 10-12 hours

Servings: 2-4

Ingredients:

2 T. vegetable oil

2 lbs. beef round steak

½ C. flour

3 to 4 potatoes

4 large carrots

2 onions

½ tsp. salt

½ tsp. pepper

1 (14½ oz.) can diced tomatoes in juice

1 (8 oz.) can tomato sauce

In a large skillet over medium heat, place vegetable oil. Cut beef round steak into serving size pieces. In a medium bowl, place flour. Add steak pieces and toss until evenly coated. Add coated steak pieces to skillet and cook until evenly browned.

Peel and quarter the potatoes. Cut carrots and onions into ½" thick slices. Place vegetables across bottom of slow cooker and set browned steak pieces over vegetables. Sprinkle salt and pepper over ingredients.

In a separate bowl, combine diced tomatoes in juice and tomato sauce. Mix well and pour over ingredients in slow cooker. Cover and cook on low setting for 10 to 12 hours.

Beef Bourguignon

Prep Time: 15-20 minutes

Cook Time: 10-12 hours

Servings: 6-8

Ingredients:

6 strips bacon

1 (3 lb.) beef rump roast

1 large carrot

1 medium onion

1 tsp. salt

½ tsp. pepper

3 T. flour

1 (10 oz.) can beef broth

2 C. red or Burgundy wine

1 T. tomato paste

2 cloves garlic, minced

½ tsp. dried thyme

1 bay leaf

½ lb. small white onions, peeled

1 lb. fresh mushrooms, sliced

Cut bacon into 1 to 2" pieces and cut beef roast into 1" cubes. In a large skillet over medium heat, cook bacon pieces until crispy. Remove from skillet and drain bacon on paper towels. Place beef cubes in skillet and cook until well browned. Remove browned beef cubes and place in slow cooker.

Peel and slice carrot and cut medium onion into slices. Place carrot and onion slices in hot skillet and sauté until browned. Season carrot and onion mixture with salt and pepper. Stir in flour and beef broth. Mix well and transfer mixture to slow cooker.

Add cooked bacon, red wine, tomato paste, minced garlic, thyme, bay leaf, peeled white onions and sliced mushrooms to slow cooker. Cover and cook on low setting for 10 to 12 hours.

Pot Roast & Veggies

Prep Time: 15 minutes

Cook Time: 10-12 hours

Servings: 6-8

Ingredients:

1 (2 to 2½ lb.) boneless beef round or chuck roast

1 tsp. garlic powder

1 T. vegetable oil

4 medium potatoes

3 C. fresh or frozen baby carrots

1 medium onion

2 tsp. dried basil

2 (10¼ oz.) cans beef gravy

Trim excess fat from beef roast and season all sides with garlic powder. In a medium skillet over medium high heat, place vegetable oil. Place roast in skillet and brown all sides.

Cut each potato into 6 wedges and cut onion into thick slices. Place potato wedges, onion slices and baby carrots across bottom of slow cooker. Sprinkle dried basil over vegetables. Place seasoned roast over vegetables in slow cooker. Pour beef gravy over all.

Cover and cook on low setting for 10 to 12 hours. To serve, remove roast from slow cooker and place on a serving platter. Place cooked vegetables around roast on platter and spoon gravy over all. Let roast stand for about 10 minutes before slicing.

Corned Beef & Cabbage

Prep Time: 10 minutes

Cook Time: 10-12 hours

Servings: 6

Ingredients:

4 lbs. corned beef

1 cabbage

4 medium golden potatoes

1 small carrot

1 stalk celery

2 tsp. prepared horseradish

2 tsp. dry mustard

2 T. molasses

1 (12 oz.) can or bottle dark beer

Trim excess fat from corned beef. Cut cabbage in eighths. Peel potatoes and carrot. Chop potatoes into 1" cubes. Cut carrot and celery into 2" pieces. Place vegetables across bottom of slow cooker.

In a small bowl, whisk together horseradish, dry mustard and molasses. Mix well and rub mixture over corned beef. Place seasoned corned beef over vegetables in slow cooker. Pour beer over ingredients.

Cover and cook on low setting for 10 to 12 hours. To serve, remove vegetables and corned beef to a serving platter. Drizzle liquid from slow cooker over all.

Zesty Italian Pot Roast

Prep Time: 10-15 minutes

Cook Time: 10-12 hours

Servings: 4-6

Ingredients:

4 medium potatoes

1 stalk celery

2 C. fresh or frozen baby carrots

1 medium plum tomato, diced

1 (2½ lb.) boneless beef round or chuck roast

½ tsp. pepper

1 (10¾ oz.) can tomato soup

½ C. water

1 T. minced garlic or roasted chopped garlic

1 tsp. dried basil

1 tsp. dried oregano

1 tsp. parsley flakes

1 tsp. vinegar

Cut each potato into quarters and slice celery into 1" pieces. Place quartered potatoes, sliced celery, baby carrots and diced tomatoes in slow cooker. Season beef roast with pepper and place over vegetables in slow cooker.

In a medium bowl, combine tomato soup, water, garlic, dried basil, dried oregano, dried parsley flakes and vinegar. Mix until well combined and pour over roast and vegetables in slow cooker.

Cover and cook on low setting for 10 to 12 hours. To serve, remove roast from slow cooker and place on a serving platter. Place cooked vegetables around roast on platter. Let roast stand for about 10 minutes before slicing.

Beef n' Gravy

Prep Time: 5 minutes

Cook Time: 10-12 hours

Servings: 8

Ingredients:

1 (3 lb.) beef roast, cubed

1 env. dry onion soup mix

½ C. beef broth

1 (10¾ oz.) can cream of mushroom soup

1 (4 oz.) can sliced mushrooms, drained

Cut beef roast into desired sized cubes. Place cubed meat in slow cooker. Sprinkle dry onion soup mix over cubed beef. Add beef broth, cream of mushroom soup and drained sliced mushrooms. Using a long spoon, mix ingredients until well combined.

Cover and cook on low setting for 10 to 12 hours. To serve, remove meat and mushrooms to a serving platter. Spoon gravy over meat and serve immediately.

Sauerbraten

Prep Time: 10 minutes

Cook Time: 10-12 hours

Servings: 6-8

Ingredients:

1 (3 to 4 lb.) beef rump roast

1½ tsp. salt

½ tsp. pepper

1 large onion

1 small cabbage

3 medium potatoes

1 bay leaf

½ C. red wine vinegar

¼ C. water

1 beef bouillon cube

Trim excess fat from beef rump roast and season with salt and pepper. Coarsely chop the onion. Cut cabbage into eighths and quarter each potato. Place vegetables across bottom of slow cooker.

Place seasoned rump roast over vegetables. Add bay leaf, red wine vinegar, water and beef bouillon cube. Cover and cook on low setting for 10 to 12 hours. To serve, remove meat and vegetables to a serving platter. Let roast cool slightly before cutting into slices.

Mexican Pot Roast

Prep Time: 15 minutes

Cook Time: 10-12 hours

Servings: 6-8

Ingredients:

2 T. vegetable oil

1 (3 lb.) beef brisket, cubed

½ C. slivered almonds

2 C. mild or hot Picante sauce

2 T. vinegar

1 tsp. garlic powder

½ tsp. salt

¼ tsp. cinnamon

¼ tsp. dried thyme

¼ tsp. dried oregano

⅛ tsp. ground cloves

⅛ tsp. pepper

½ to ¾ C. water

In a large skillet over medium high heat, place vegetable oil. Place cubed beef in skillet and heat until browned. Place browned cubed meat in slow cooker.

In a medium bowl, combine slivered almonds, Picante sauce, vinegar, garlic powder and salt. Add cinnamon, dried thyme, dried oregano, ground cloves and pepper. Mix until well combined and pour over browned meat in slow cooker.

Cover and cook on low setting for 10 to 12 hours. If roast seems too dry, add water as needed. To serve, remove roast from slow cooker and place on a serving platter. Let cool for about 10 minutes before slicing.

French Dip Roast

Prep Time: 5-10 minutes

Cook Time: 10-12 hours

Servings: 8-10

Ingredients:

1 large onion

1 (3 lb.) beef bottom roast

½ C. dry white wine or water

1 pkg. dry au jus gravy mix

2 C. beef broth

8 to 10 French rolls or
   long buns

Cut onion into slices and separate slices into individual rings. Place onion slices across bottom of slow cooker. Set roast over onion slices.

In a medium bowl, combine white wine and au jus gravy mix. Mix until well combined and pour over roast. Add enough beef broth to cover roast.

Cover and cook on low setting for 10 to 12 hours. To serve, remove meat and onions from liquid and let stand for 5 minutes. Slice beef across the grain into thin slices. Divide sliced meat and onions onto French rolls and drizzle some of the liquid from slow cooker over meat on each sandwich. Ladle remaining liquid into individual bowls or ramekins and serve with sandwiches for dipping.

Braised Short Ribs

Prep Time: 10-15 minutes

Cook Time: 10-12 hours

Servings: 6-8

Ingredients:

1 tsp. salt

¼ tsp. pepper

¼ C. flour

2½ lbs. beef short ribs, cut into 2 to 3 rib sections

1 to 2 T. vegetable oil

1 onion, sliced

¼ C. steak sauce

½ C. water

2 T. Worcestershire sauce

1 bay leaf

2 beef bouillon cubes

In a small bowl, combine salt, pepper and flour. Mix well and dust mixture lightly over short ribs. In a medium sauté pan over medium heat, place vegetable oil. Lightly brown ribs in pan and place browned ribs in slow cooker. Separate onion slices into rings and place over ribs in slow cooker.

Pour steak sauce, water and Worcestershire sauce over ribs and onions. Add bay leaf and beef bouillon cubes.

Cover and cook on low setting for 10 to 12 hours. To serve, remove ribs from slow cooker using long tongs. Place ribs and onions on a serving platter and spoon remaining sauce mixture over top.

Smokey Brisket

Prep Time: 5-10 minutes

Cook Time: 10-12 hours

Servings: 8-10

Ingredients:

2 medium onions

1 T. smoke-flavored salt

1 (3 to 4 lb.) beef brisket

1 tsp. celery seed

1 T. mustard seed

½ tsp. pepper

1 (12 oz.) bottle chili sauce

Cut onions into slices and separate slices into individual rings. Place onion slices across bottom of slow cooker. Sprinkle smoke-flavored salt over both sides of beef brisket. Set beef brisket in slow cooker.

In a small bowl, combine celery seed, mustard seed, pepper and chili sauce. Mix until well combined and pour mixture over beef brisket in slow cooker.

Cover and cook on low setting for 10 to 12 hours. To serve, remove brisket and onions and place on serving platter. Drizzle remaining sauce from slow cooker over brisket.

16

Italian Beef

Prep Time: 5-10 minutes

Cook Time 10-12 hours

Servings: 6-8

Ingredients:

1 (3 to 4 lb.) lean rump roast

2 tsp. salt, divided

4 cloves garlic

2 tsp. grated Romano or
Parmesan cheese, divided

1 (12 oz.) can beef broth

1 tsp. dried oregano

Set rump roast in slow cooker. Using a sharp knife, cut four 1½" to 2" deep slits into top of roast. Sprinkle ¼ teaspoon salt into each cut. Place 1 garlic clove in each cut and sprinkle ½ teaspoon cheese over garlic in each cut.

Pour beef broth over roast and sprinkle with dried oregano. Cover and cook on low setting for 10 to 12 hours. To serve, remove roast from slow cooker. Cut roast into slices or shred meat. Divide shredded meat on buns. Ladle remaining liquid into individual bowls or ramekins and serve with sandwiches for dipping.

Roast in Mushroom Sauce

Prep Time: 5-10 minutes

Cook Time: 10-12 hours

Servings: 5-6

Ingredients:

1 (1½ lb.) boneless beef chuck or rump roast

4 medium potatoes

1 (16 oz.) pkg. frozen baby carrots

1 (4 oz.) can mushroom pieces, drained

½ tsp. dried basil or tarragon

¼ tsp. salt

1 (10¾ oz.) can cream of mushroom soup

Trim excess fat from beef roast. Cut each potato into quarters. Place quartered potatoes, frozen baby carrots and drained mushroom pieces across bottom of slow cooker. Sprinkle with basil and salt.

Set beef roast over vegetables in slow cooker. Pour cream of mushroom soup over roast.

Cover and cook on low setting for 10 to 12 hours. To serve, remove roast to a serving platter. Using a slotted spoon, remove vegetables and place around roast on platter. Ladle mushroom sauce from slow cooker over roast and cut roast into slices.

Brisket & Beer

Prep Time: 10 minutes

Cook Time: 10-12 hours

Servings: 6

Ingredients:

1 onion

1 stalk celery

2 medium parsnips

½ C. chili sauce

1½ tsp. salt

¼ tsp. pepper

1 (3½ lb.) lean beef brisket

1 (12 oz.) can or bottle beer

Peel and coarsely chop the onion. Cut celery into 1" pieces. Peel and cut parsnips into 1" pieces. Layer vegetables across bottom of slow cooker.

In a medium bowl, combine chili sauce, salt and pepper. Mix well and rub mixture over beef brisket. Place brisket over vegetables in slow cooker. Pour beer over ingredients.

Cover and cook on low setting for 10 to 12 hours.

Meat Loaf Veggie Dinner

Prep Time: 10-15 minutes

Cook Time: 10-12 hours

Servings: 6-8

Ingredients:

½ C. milk

¾ C. breadcrumbs or quick cooking oats

3 medium potatoes

1 large onion

1 large carrot

2 stalks celery

2 eggs

2 lbs. lean ground beef

½ C. finely chopped onions

1 tsp. salt

¼ tsp. pepper

¾ tsp. paprika

¾ C. water

In a large bowl, combine milk and breadcrumbs. Set aside and let soak. Meanwhile, cut potatoes into quarters and coarsely chop the onion, carrot and celery stalks.

Add eggs to bread-crumb mixture. Mix until well combined and add ground beef, ½ cup finely chopped onions, salt, pepper and paprika. Knead mixture by hand until well combined.

Place mixture in a greased loaf pan or other heat-safe dish that will fit inside the slow cooker. Place vegetables across bottom of slow cooker. Pour water over vegetables and set loaf pan over vegetables in slow cooker.

Cover and cook on low setting for 10 to 12 hours. Use a hot pad to carefully remove loaf pan from slow cooker. Pour excess fat from top of loaf before turning out onto a serving platter. Allow loaf to cool slightly before slicing. Serve with cooked vegetables.

Beef in Red Wine

Prep Time: 10-15 minutes

Cook Time: 10-12 hours

Servings: 6

Ingredients:

1½ lbs. beef stew meat

2 medium onions, chopped

2 beef bouillon cubes or 1 env.
dry onion soup mix

3 T. cornstarch

Salt and pepper to taste

1½ C. dry red wine

Prepared whole wheat pasta,
optional

Trim excess fat from beef and cut meat into 1" cubes. Place beef cubes and chopped onions in slow cooker. Crumble bouillon cubes or sprinkle onion soup mix over meat and onions. Sprinkle cornstarch, salt and pepper over ingredients in slow cooker.

Pour red wine over all. Cover and cook on low setting for 10 to 12 hours. If desired, serve beef and onions over prepared whole wheat pasta. Ladle some of the remaining liquid from slow cooker over beef.

BBQ Beef Sandwiches

Prep Time: 10-15 minutes

Cook Time: 10-12 hours

Servings: 12-16

Ingredients:

1 (4 lb.) beef round steak

1 C. chopped onions

½ C. brown sugar

1 T. chili powder

2 cloves garlic, minced

2 carrots, finely chopped

½ C. ketchup

⅓ C. apple cider vinegar

1 (12 oz.) can or bottle beer

1 (6 oz.) can tomato paste

12 to 16 hamburger buns
   or rolls

Trim excess fat from beef round steak and cut into 1" pieces. Place beef pieces in slow cooker. Add chopped onions, brown sugar, chili powder, minced garlic and chopped carrots to slow cooker. Stir in ketchup, apple cider vinegar, beer and tomato paste. Using a long spoon, mix all together until well combined.

Cover and cook on low setting for 10 to 12 hours, or until beef is very tender. If desired, beef can be shredded by removing beef cubes to a plate and pulling meat apart with two forks. Return shredded meat to sauce in slow cooker and mix well. To serve, use a slotted spoon to place barbequed beef on hamburger buns.

Sweet & Sour Meatballs

Prep Time: 35 minutes

Cook Time: 10-12 hours

Servings: 4-6

Ingredients:

1 lb. ground beef

½ C. dry breadcrumbs

¼ C. milk

2 T. chopped onions

1 tsp. salt

½ tsp. Worcestershire sauce

1 egg, beaten

1 (20 oz.) can pineapple
   chunks

½ C. brown sugar

⅓ C. apple cider vinegar

1 T. soy sauce

1 T. cornstarch

1 small green pepper

Preheat oven to 350°. In a large bowl, combine ground beef, dry breadcrumbs, milk, chopped onions, salt, Worcestershire sauce and beaten egg. Mix by hand until well combined. Form mixture into 1½" meatballs. Place meatballs on a baking sheet and bake in oven for 20 to 25 minutes, or until cooked throughout. Place cooked meatballs in slow cooker.

Drain pineapple chunks, reserving the juice. In a medium saucepan over medium heat, combine reserved pineapple juice, brown sugar, apple cider vinegar and soy sauce. Mix well and stir in cornstarch. Bring mixture to a boil and pour over meatballs in slow cooker.

Slice green pepper into long, thin strips. Carefully stir green pepper strips and pineapple chunks into slow cooker. Cover and cook on low setting for 10 to 12 hours. To serve, remove meatballs to a serving platter and spoon sauce with pineapple chunks and green pepper strips over meatballs.

Shredded Beef & Jalapenos

Prep Time: 15 minutes

Cook Time: 10-12 hours

Servings: 8-10

Ingredients:

1 (5 lb.) beef chuck roast

3 cloves garlic, crushed

1 T. paprika

1 T. celery salt

1 T. garlic powder

1 T. parsley flakes

½ T. pepper

½ T. chili powder

½ T. cayenne pepper

½ tsp. seasoned salt

½ tsp. dry mustard

½ tsp. dried tarragon

4 oz. beer

1½ T. Worcestershire sauce

4 T. hot pepper sauce

2 tsp. liquid smoke flavoring

1 large onion, chopped

1 green bell pepper, chopped

2 jalapeno peppers,
  seeded and
  chopped

8 to 10 hamburger
  buns

Trim excess fat from chuck roast. Using a sharp knife, poke 1" deep holes in several places on surface of roast. Press some of the crushed garlic into each hole.

In a small bowl, combine paprika, celery salt, garlic powder, dried parsley, pepper, chili powder, cayenne pepper, seasoned salt, dry mustard and dried tarragon. Mix until well combined. Rub mixture entirely over surface of roast. Place roast in slow cooker.

In a medium bowl, combine beer, Worcestershire sauce, hot pepper sauce and liquid smoke flavoring. Mix well and pour liquid over roast in slow cooker. Place chopped onion, chopped green pepper and chopped jalapenos around roast.

Cover and cook on low setting for 10 to 12 hours. Shred beef by removing roast to a platter and pulling meat apart with two forks. Return shredded meat to slow cooker and mix well. To serve, use a slotted spoon to place shredded beef, onions and peppers on hamburger buns.

24

CHICKEN

Roast Chicken

Prep Time: 10-15 minutes

Cook Time: 10-12 hours

Servings: 6-8

Ingredients:

1 medium onion

2 stalks celery

1 large carrot

1 bay leaf

1 small bunch parsley

¾ C. water

1 (6½ lb.) roasting chicken

Salt and pepper to taste

¼ C. butter, melted

Coarsely chop the onion, celery stalks and carrot. Place chopped vegetables across bottom of slow cooker. Add bay leaf and parsley bunch, including sprigs and leaves. Pour water over vegetables.

Thoroughly wash chicken and pat dry with paper towels. Sprinkle salt and pepper inside chicken cavity. If desired, fold legs and wings of chicken across chicken breast and secure with kitchen string. Place chicken breast-side-down in slow cooker. Using a pastry brush, spread melted butter over chicken. Sprinkle salt and pepper entirely over outer chicken skin.

Cover and cook on low setting for 10 to 12 hours. To serve, remove roast chicken to a serving platter and, if necessary, remove kitchen string. Spoon vegetables around chicken on platter. Let cool slightly before slicing chicken.

Chicken & Mushrooms

Prep Time: 10 minutes

Cook Time: 10-12 hours

Servings: 6

Ingredients:

6 frozen boneless, skinless chicken breast halves

2 (10¾ oz.) cans cream of chicken soup

1 (4 oz.) can sliced mushrooms

¾ tsp. salt

¼ tsp. pepper

Prepared white rice

Set frozen chicken breast halves in slow cooker.

In a medium bowl, combine cream of chicken soup, sliced mushrooms, salt and pepper. Mix until well combined. Pour mixture over chicken in slow cooker.

Cover and cook on low setting for 10 to 12 hours. To serve, divide prepared rice onto serving plates. Place one cooked chicken breast over rice on each plate. Spoon mushroom sauce from slow cooker over each serving.

Creamy Chicken & Veggies

Prep Time: 10-15 minutes

Cook Time: 10-12 hours, plus 15 minutes

Servings: 6

Ingredients:

1 (4 lb.) whole chicken

2 lbs. small red potatoes

1 (16 oz.) pkg. baby carrots

1 onion, chopped

2 cloves garlic, minced

1 (14 oz.) can chicken broth

1 C. sour cream

3 T. flour

⅛ tsp. white pepper

½ tsp. dried thyme

Cut chicken into individual pieces, such as legs, wings and breast. Cut potatoes in half. Place potatoes, carrots, chopped onion and minced garlic across bottom of slow cooker. Place chicken pieces over vegetables. Pour chicken broth over ingredients in slow cooker.

Cover and cook on low setting for 10 to 12 hours. In a small bowl, combine sour cream, flour, white pepper and dried thyme, mixing until well blended. Increase slow cooker to high setting and stir sour cream mixture into vegetables and chicken in slow cooker. Cover and cook for an additional 15 to 20 minutes, stirring occasionally, until sauce is thickened.

To serve, remove chicken pieces to a serving platter. Place vegetables around chicken on platter and spoon sauce from slow cooker over all.

40 Clove Garlic Chicken

Prep Time: 10-15 minutes

Cook Time: 10-12 hours

Servings: 6-8

Ingredients:

2 stalks celery

1 (4 lb.) fryer chicken

3 T. olive oil

1 tsp. dried thyme

1 tsp. dried sage

1 tsp. salt

½ tsp. dried rosemary

½ tsp. pepper

½ C. chicken broth

⅓ C. dry white wine

3 heads garlic

1 loaf French bread

Coarsely chop celery and place across bottom of slow cooker. Remove neck and gizzards from fryer chicken. Thoroughly rinse and clean chicken and pat completely dry. Place lemon quarters inside chicken cavity. Rub olive oil all over outer chicken skin.

In a small bowl, combine dried thyme, dried sage, salt, dried rosemary and pepper. Mix well and sprinkle seasoning mixture over chicken. Place seasoned chicken over celery in slow cooker. Pour chicken broth and dry white wine around chicken.

Separate garlic into individual cloves, but do not peel the cloves. Place cloves all around chicken. Cover and cook on low setting for 10 to 12 hours. To serve, remove chicken to a serving platter and let cool slightly before slicing. Serve with toasted French bread. Squeeze roasted garlic from skins and spread lightly over

Chicken Pot Pie

Prep Time: 10-15 minutes

Cook Time: 10-11 hours, plus 20 minutes

Servings: 8-10

Ingredients:

2 lbs. boneless chicken meat

1⅔ C. flour, divided

1¾ tsp. salt, divided

½ tsp. pepper

½ tsp. paprika

2 carrots, chopped

2 stalks celery, chopped

1 large onion, chopped

2 medium potatoes, chopped

¾ C. frozen peas

¾ C. frozen corn

2 C. chicken broth

1 C. cornmeal

1 T. baking powder

2 T. sugar

¼ C. butter

1 egg

1 C. milk

Cut chicken meat into 1" to 2" cubes. In a bowl, combine ⅓ cup flour, 1 teaspoon salt, pepper and paprika. Mix well and add cubed chicken. Toss until chicken is completely coated. Combine carrots, celery, onion, potatoes, frozen peas and frozen corn. Place chopped vegetables and coated chicken pieces in slow cooker. Add chicken broth and mix all until well combined.

Cover and cook on low setting for 10 to 11 hours. Then, increase slow cooker to high and preheat oven to 400°. In a small bowl, combine ⅓ cup flour with ⅓ cup water. Mix well and add to mixture in slow cooker, stirring until well incorporated.

To prepare cornbread topping, in a large bowl, combine remaining 1 cup flour, cornmeal, baking powder, sugar and remaining ¾ teaspoon salt. Using a pastry blender, cut in butter. Stir in egg and milk until a thick batter forms. Pour mixture over ingredients in slow cooker. Remove stoneware dish from slow cooker and place directly on oven rack. Bake in oven for 20 minutes, or until topping is lightly browned.

Florida Chicken

Prep Time: 10 minutes

Cook Time 10-12 hours

Servings: 8-10

Ingredients:

1 (10 oz.) can Spanish-style vegetable soup

½ C. orange juice

2 T. honey

¼ C. chicken broth

2 T. fresh lemon or lime juice

½ tsp. minced gingerroot

1 clove garlic, minced

1 tsp. dried chives

1 tsp. parsley flakes

3 lbs. frozen chicken parts or frozen chicken breasts

In a medium bowl, whisk together vegetable soup, orange juice, honey, chicken broth, lemon juice, minced gingerroot, minced garlic, dried chives and parsley flakes. Mix until well combined. Ladle some of the liquid mixture into bottom of slow cooker.

Place some of the frozen chicken parts over sauce and top with additional sauce. Add more chicken parts and top with additional sauce. Continue layering until all chicken parts and sauce have been used.

Cover and cook on low setting for 10 to 12 hours. To serve, remove chicken to a serving platter or individual plates. Spoon additional sauce from slow cooker over each serving.

Chicken á la King

Prep Time: 10 minutes

Cook Time: 10-12 hours

Servings: 6-8

Ingredients:

2 lbs. chicken breast or tenders

1 lb. smoked sausage

1 medium onion

1 red bell pepper

1 green bell pepper

2 stalks celery

1 (10 oz.) can cream of chicken soup

1 (10 oz.) can cream of mushroom soup

1½ C. milk

Chicken broth, optional

Prepared biscuits, split

Cut chicken into 1" to 2" cubes and cut smoked sausage into 1" slices. Coarsely chop the onion, bell peppers and celery. Place chopped vegetables, cubed chicken and sliced smoked sausage in slow cooker.

In a medium bowl, whisk together cream of chicken soup, cream of mushroom soup and milk, mixing until well combined. Pour soup mixture over ingredients in slow cooker.

Cover and cook on low setting for 10 to 12 hours. If needed, stir a little chicken broth into slow cooker to thin mixture before serving. To serve, place split biscuits on serving plates and ladle chicken and vegetables over biscuits.

Chicken Elizabeth

Prep Time: 10 minutes

Cook Time: 10-12 hours, plus 10 minutes

Servings: 6-8

Ingredients:

1 (10 oz.) can cream of asparagus soup

1 tsp. dried thyme

½ tsp. paprika

1 tsp. minced garlic

¾ C. chicken broth

2½ lbs. frozen chicken breasts

¾ C. sour cream

1 C. crumbled bleu cheese

Prepared white rice

In a small bowl, whisk together cream of asparagus soup, dried thyme, paprika, minced garlic and chicken broth. Ladle some of the soup mixture into bottom of slow cooker.

Place some of the frozen chicken breasts over sauce and top with additional sauce. Add more chicken breasts and top with additional sauce. Continue layering until all chicken and sauce have been used.

Cover and cook on low setting for 10 to 12 hours. Then, increase slow cooker to high setting. In a small bowl, combine sour cream and bleu cheese. Pour sour cream mixture over chicken. Cover and cook for an additional 10 minutes, or until sauce is heated throughout. To serve, place chicken on serving plates and ladle sauce from slow cooker over each serving. If desired, serve with prepared rice.

Hot Chicken Salad

Prep Time: 15 minutes

Cook Time: 10-11 hours

Servings: 6

Ingredients:

2 lbs. chicken breasts or tenders

2 stalks celery, chopped

1 C. slivered almonds

1 tsp. salt

½ tsp. dried thyme

¼ tsp. pepper

1 C. prepared brown rice

⅓ C. Italian dressing

¼ C. chicken broth

Mayonnaise, optional

Cut chicken breasts or tenders into 1" cubes. In a large bowl, combine cubed chicken, chopped celery, slivered almonds, salt, dried thyme and pepper. Mix until well combined. Add prepared brown rice, Italian dressing and chicken broth. Toss all together until evenly incorporated.

Transfer mixture to slow cooker. Cover and cook on low setting for 10 to 11 hours. To serve, mix salad lightly before spooning onto serving plates. If desired, mix a little mayonnaise into each serving.

One-Dish Chicken Dinner

Prep Time: 15-20 minutes

Cook Time: 10-12 hours

Servings: 6

Ingredients:

2 medium carrots

1 medium cabbage

1 (10 oz.) pkg. frozen pearl onions

2 lbs. small red potatoes, halved

¼ C. butter

6 chicken breasts

Salt and pepper to taste

⅓ C. plus ¼ C. flour, divided

1¾ C. apple juice

Coarsely chop the carrots and cabbage. Place half of the chopped carrots, half of the chopped cabbage, half of the frozen pearl onions and half of the potatoes in slow cooker.

In a medium skillet over medium heat, melt butter. Season chicken breasts with salt and pepper to taste. In a medium shallow bowl, place ⅓ cup flour. Dredge chicken breasts in flour until evenly coated. Place coated chicken breasts in skillet and heat, turning once, until lightly browned. Place chicken over vegetables in slow cooker. Place remaining vegetables over chicken.

In a medium bowl, combine apple juice and remaining ¼ cup flour, mixing until well combined. Pour mixture over ingredients in slow cooker. Cover and cook on low setting for 10 to 12 hours.

Coq au Vin

Prep Time: 20 minutes

Cook Time: 10-12 hours

Servings: 6-8

Ingredients:

1 (10 oz.) pkg. frozen pearl onions

1 C. baby carrots

6 small red potatoes, halved

½ lb. mushrooms, halved

1 stalk celery, chopped

2 cloves garlic, minced

1 tsp. salt

¼ tsp. pepper

½ tsp. dried thyme

½ tsp. dried marjoram

1 bay leaf

2 slices bacon, chopped

3 lbs. chicken leg quarters

½ C. chicken broth

2 T. tomato paste

1½ C. dry white wine

In a large bowl, place frozen pearl onions, baby carrots, halved red potatoes, halved mushrooms, chopped celery and minced garlic. Sprinkle salt, pepper, dried thyme and dried marjoram over vegetables. Toss until vegetables are evenly seasoned. Place half of the vegetables in slow cooker. Add bay leaf.

In a medium skillet over medium high heat, cook chopped bacon until crisp. Remove bacon from skillet and drain on paper towels. Add cooked bacon to slow cooker. Place chicken leg quarters in skillet, turning once, until lightly browned. Place chicken in slow cooker and top with remaining seasoned vegetables.

In a medium bowl, whisk together chicken broth and tomato paste. Stir in dry white wine. Pour mixture over ingredients in slow cooker. Cover and cook on low setting for 10 to 12 hours. To serve, remove vegetables and chicken to a serving platter.

Chicken & Braised Carrots

Prep Time: 15-20 minutes

Cook Time: 10-12 hours

Servings: 6-8

Ingredients:

1 (4 to 5 lb.) roasting chicken

1 tsp. salt

½ tsp. pepper

1 medium onion, sliced

2 lbs. baby carrots

2 T. butter, melted

⅓ C. orange juice

2 tsp. grated orange peel

3 T. honey

2 tsp. apple cider vinegar

Remove neck and gizzards from roasting chicken. Thoroughly rinse and clean chicken and pat completely dry. Season chicken with salt and pepper.

Place onion slices across bottom of slow cooker. Set chicken over onion slices and arrange baby carrots around chicken.

In a small bowl, whisk together melted butter, orange juice, grated orange peel, honey and apple cider vinegar. Pour mixture over ingredients in slow cooker.

Cover and cook on low setting for 10 to 12 hours. To serve, remove chicken to a serving platter. Arrange cooked carrots and onions around chicken. Let chicken cool slightly before slicing.

Parmagiana Chicken

Prep Time: 15-20 minutes

Cook Time: 10-12 hours

Servings: 3-6

Ingredients:

¼ C. olive oil

3 (¾ lb. each) large butterfly chicken breasts

Salt and pepper to taste

1 egg, lightly beaten

1 C. fine breadcrumbs

1 large eggplant

2 C. marinara sauce, divided

6 slices deli ham

¾ to 1 C. shredded mozzarella cheese

Grated Parmesan cheese

In a skillet over medium heat, place olive oil. Season chicken breasts with salt and pepper to taste. Place lightly beaten egg and fine breadcrumbs in two separate bowls. Dip seasoned chicken breasts first into the egg and then into the breadcrumbs. Place coated chicken breasts in skillet and heat until lightly browned.

Cut eggplant into ½" slices. Pour ½ cup marinara sauce across bottom of slow cooker. Place one chicken breast in slow cooker and top with 2 ham slices and ⅓ of the sliced eggplant. Top with another chicken breast, 2 ham slices and ⅓ of the eggplant. Repeat layers again with final chicken breast, remaining 2 ham slices and remaining eggplant. Pour remaining 1½ cups marinara sauce over all.

Cover and cook on low setting for 10 to 12 hours. During last 15 minutes of cooking time, increase slow cooker to high setting. Sprinkle mozzarella cheese over all, cover and cook for an additional 15 minutes, or until cheese is melted. Remove chicken, ham and eggplant to a serving platter. Sprinkle desired amount of Parmesan cheese over all.

Chicken Cacciatore

Prep Time: 10 minutes

Cook Time: 10-12 hours

Servings: 4-6

Ingredients:

2 medium onions, thinly sliced

2½ to 3 lbs. frozen chicken breasts

1 tsp. salt

¼ tsp. pepper

3 cloves garlic, minced

1 (28 oz.) can crushed tomatoes, drained

1 (8 oz.) can tomato sauce

2 tsp. dried oregano

1 tsp. dried basil

¼ C. dry white wine

1 bay leaf

Prepared pasta, optional

Place onion slices across bottom of slow cooker. Season frozen chicken breasts lightly with salt and pepper. Place seasoned chicken breasts over onions.

In a medium bowl, combine minced garlic, crushed tomatoes, tomato sauce, dried oregano, dried basil and dry white wine. Mix until well combined and pour over chicken in slow cooker. Add bay leaf.

Cover and cook on low setting for 10 to 12 hours. To serve, remove chicken breasts to serving plates and spoon remaining tomato sauce from slow cooker over each serving. If desired, serve with prepared pasta.

Chicken in Orange Sauce

Prep Time: 10 minutes

Cook Time: 10-12 hours

Servings: 6-8

Ingredients:

4 lbs. chicken parts

2 tsp. salt

1 ½ tsp. paprika

½ tsp. pepper

2 large carrots

3 stalks celery

½ lb. mushrooms, halved

2 T. brown sugar

½ tsp. ground ginger

1 (6 oz.) can frozen orange juice concentrate, thawed

Season chicken parts with salt, paprika and pepper. Cut carrots and celery into 1" pieces. Arrange carrot pieces, celery pieces and halved mushrooms across bottom of slow cooker. Place seasoned chicken parts over vegetables.

In a medium bowl, combine brown sugar, ground ginger and orange juice concentrate. Mix until well combined and pour over chicken and vegetables in slow cooker.

Cover and cook on low setting for 10 to 12 hours.

Fricassee Chicken

Prep Time: 15-20 minutes

Cook Time: 10-12 hours,
plus 10 minutes

Servings: 6-8

Ingredients:

4 T. butter

4 lbs. chicken parts

Salt and pepper to taste

1 large onion, chopped

⅓ C. flour

3 C. hot water

3 chicken bouillon cubes

3 carrots

3 stalks celery

½ lb. mushrooms, quartered

¾ tsp. dried thyme

1 C. heavy cream or half n' half

In a medium skillet over medium heat, melt butter. Lightly season chicken parts with salt and pepper and set aside. Place chicken parts in skillet, turning once, until lightly browned. Remove chicken from skillet and set aside. Add chopped onion to skillet and sauté for 1 minute. Add flour to skillet and mix well. Stir in hot water and bouillon. Using a wire whisk, mix ingredients until a light gravy forms.

Coarsely chop carrots and celery. Place chopped carrots, chopped celery, quartered mushrooms and dried thyme in slow cooker. Place chicken parts over vegetables in slow cooker. Pour gravy mixture over all.

Cover and cook on low setting for 10 to 12 hours. Before serving, stir heavy cream into mixture, cover and cook for an additional 10 minutes. Stir lightly before removing chicken and vegetables to a platter. Spoon remaining sauce mixture from slow cooker over all.

Stuffed Chicken

Prep Time: 15-20 minutes

Cook Time: 10-12 hours

Servings: 6-8

Ingredients:

1 (3½ to 4 lb.) fryer chicken

2½ C. dry cubed cornbread

¼ tsp. dried thyme

¼ tsp. pepper

1 C. cooked ground breakfast sausage

4 T. butter, divided

½ C. chopped celery

½ C. chopped onions

1 C. chicken broth, warmed

Salt, pepper and paprika to taste

Remove neck and gizzards from roasting chicken, reserving gizzards. Rinse and clean chicken inside and out and pat dry. Dice gizzards.

In a bowl, combine gizzards, cornbread cubes, thyme, pepper and cooked sausage. In a skillet over medium heat, melt 1 tablespoon butter. Add celery and onions and sauté for 1 to 2 minutes. Add vegetables to sausage mixture. Pour chicken broth over mixture and toss all together. Let stuffing cool completely. Stuff cleaned chicken with mixture and, if desired, tie opening to enclose stuffing. Be sure not to overstuff the chicken. Set chicken in slow cooker. In a small bowl, melt remaining butter. Brush butter over chicken and season with salt, pepper and paprika.

Cover and cook on low setting for 10 to 12 hours. To serve, remove chicken to a platter. Using a meat thermometer, test the stuffing temperature. If stuffing has not reached at least 165° F, immediately remove stuffing and bake in a separate dish in oven until stuffing temperature reaches 165°. If stuffing has already reached 165°, immediately remove stuffing from chicken and serve on the side.

Basque Chicken

Prep Time: 10-15 minutes

Cook Time: 10-12 hours

Servings: 6

Ingredients:

½ lb. sliced ham, cut into strips

1½ to 2 lbs. red and yellow bell peppers, chopped

1 large onion, chopped

4 small jalapenos, seeded and chopped

12 cloves garlic, chopped

¾ tsp. salt

½ tsp. pepper

3 lbs. frozen chicken breasts

1 (28 oz.) can whole tomatoes in juice

2 T. tomato paste

3 T. olive oil

Prepared rice, optional

Toasted French bread, optional

In a medium bowl, combine ham strips, chopped bell peppers, chopped onion, chopped jalapenos, chopped garlic, salt and pepper. Mix until well combined. Spread half of the mixture across bottom of slow cooker. Place frozen chicken breasts over pepper mixture. Arrange remaining pepper mixture over chicken.

In a medium bowl, combine whole tomatoes and juice, tomato paste and olive oil. Mix until well combined and pour over ingredients in slow cooker.

Cover and cook on low setting for 10 to 12 hours. To serve, remove chicken, ham and vegetables to a serving platter. Spoon remaining sauce from slow cooker over all. If desired, serve with prepared rice and toasted French bread.

Chicken Paprikash

Prep Time: 15-20 minutes

Cook Time: 10-12 hours, plus 5 minutes

Servings: 6-8

Ingredients:

4 lbs. chicken hind quarters

Salt and pepper to taste

2 T. butter

2 large sweet onions, thinly sliced

¼ C. Sweet Hungarian paprika*

2 T. flour

1½ C. chicken broth

2 cloves garlic, minced

1 bay leaf

1½ C. sour cream

Lemon wedges

*Sweet Hungarian paprika has a sweet pepper flavor without the heat. Any paprika can be used as a substitution.

Season chicken hind quarters with salt and pepper to taste. In a medium skillet over medium heat, melt butter. Place chicken quarters in skillet, turning once, until lightly browned. Place browned chicken in slow cooker.

Add onion slices to skillet and sauté for 2 to 3 minutes. Add paprika and flour and sauté for an additional 30 seconds. Pour chicken broth over mixture and stir, using a wire whisk, until a light sauce forms. Pour sauce over chicken.

Cover and cook on low setting for 10 to 12 hours. To serve, remove chicken to a serving platter. Increase slow cooker to high setting. Stir sour cream into sauce in slow cooker. Cover and cook for an additional 5 minutes, or until sauce is heated throughout. Ladle sauce over chicken and serve with lemon wedges.

PORK

Hawaiian Pork Roast

Prep Time: 10-15 minutes

Cook Time: 10-12 hours

Servings: 6-8

Ingredients:

1 (5 lb.) loin or end pork roast

Salt and pepper to taste

1 large onion, peeled and
   sliced

1 green pepper, coarsely
   chopped

¾ C. hot water

4 T. sugar

2 T. soy sauce

2 T. sherry wine

½ tsp. ground ginger

3 T. white wine vinegar

2 T. ketchup

1 (10 oz.) can pineapple
   chunks

Trim excess fat from pork roast. Season roast with salt and pepper to taste. Place onion slices across bottom of slow cooker. Set roast over onion slices and arrange chopped green peppers around the roast.

In a medium bowl, combine hot water, sugar, soy sauce, sherry wine, ground ginger, white wine vinegar and ketchup.

Cover and cook on low setting for 10 to 12 hours. Add drained pineapple chunks during last 30 minutes of cooking time, or until pineapple is heated throughout. To serve, remove roast from slow cooker and place on a serving platter. Spoon vegetables, pineapple and remaining sauce over roast.

Pork Roast with Apples

Prep Time: 10-15 minutes

Cook Time: 10-12 hours

Servings: 6

Ingredients:

1 (5 lb.) pork shoulder roast

Salt and pepper to taste

2 to 3 Granny Smith apples, peeled

2 medium sweet potatoes, peeled

1 medium sweet onion, thinly sliced

½ C. water

¼ C. apple cider vinegar

⅓ C. brown sugar

¼ C. butter

Trim excess fat from pork roast. Season roast with salt and pepper to taste. Cut each peeled apple in eight parts and slice peeled sweet potatoes into ½" thick slices. Layer onion slices across bottom of slow cooker, followed by the sweet potatoes and finally the apple sections. Pour water and apple cider vinegar over vegetables.

Place trimmed pork shoulder roast over vegetables and sprinkle brown sugar over all. Cut butter into pieces and place pats of butter over roast and vegetables.

Cover and cook on low setting for 10 to 12 hours. To serve, remove roast from slow cooker and place on a serving platter. Spoon cooked vegetables and apples around roast on platter.

Pulled Pork Sandwiches

Prep Time: 10-15 minutes

Cook Time: 10-12 hours

Servings: 10

Ingredients:

2 onions, quartered

2 T. brown sugar

1 T. paprika

2 tsp. salt

½ tsp. pepper

1 (4 to 6 lb.) boneless pork end or shoulder roast

⅔ C. apple cider vinegar

4 tsp. Worcestershire sauce

1 tsp. red pepper flakes

1½ tsp. sugar

½ tsp. dry mustard

½ tsp. garlic salt

¼ tsp. cayenne pepper

Hamburger buns

Place quartered onions across bottom of slow cooker. In a medium bowl, combine brown sugar, paprika, salt and pepper. Mix well and rub mixture over pork roast. Place pork roast over onions in slow cooker.

In a medium bowl, combine apple cider vinegar, Worcestershire sauce, red pepper flakes, sugar, dry mustard, garlic salt and cayenne pepper. Drizzle ¼ of the vinegar mixture over roast. Cover and refrigerate remaining vinegar mixture.

Cover and cook on low setting for 10 to 12 hours. Remove roast and onions from slow cooker and drain off liquid. Chop or shred meat and onions. To serve, place shredded meat and onion mixture over hamburger buns. If desired, remaining vinegar mixture may be drizzled lightly over sandwiches.

Ham & Potatoes

Prep Time: 5 minutes

Cook Time: 10-12 hours,

Servings: 6

Ingredients:

6 to 8 medium red potatoes, cut into chunks

1 (2 to 3 lb.) boneless ham

½ C. brown sugar

1 tsp. dry mustard

Using a fork, prick holes into potato chunks. Place potatoes across bottom of slow cooker. Place boneless ham over potatoes and sprinkle brown sugar and dry mustard over ham.

Cover and cook on low setting for 10 to 12 hours, until potatoes are tender. To serve, remove ham and potatoes from slow cooker and place on a serving platter. Let ham cool slightly before slicing. Pour remaining juices from slow cooker over ham and potatoes.

Home-Style Asian Ribs

Prep Time: 5-10 minutes

Cook Time: 10 to 11 hours

Servings: 6

Ingredients:

½ C. soy sauce

¼ C. ketchup

½ C. orange marmalade

1 clove garlic, minced

2 tsp. fresh grated gingerroot

¼ tsp. cayenne pepper, optional

3½ to 4 lbs. home style pork ribs

In a medium bowl, whisk together soy sauce, ketchup, orange marmalade, minced garlic, grated gingerroot and cayenne pepper. Mix until well combined.

Using a basting brush, baste sauce mixture over each rib and place ribs in slow cooker. Pour remaining sauce over ribs. Cover and cook on low setting for 10 to 11 hours. To serve, remove ribs from slow cooker with long tongs and place on a serving platter.

Barbequed Pork

Prep Time: 10 minutes

Cook Time: 10-12 hours,
plus 30 minutes

Servings: 10

Ingredients:

3 onions, 2 sliced and
1 chopped

1 (4 to 5 lb.) pork roast or fresh
picnic ham

5 to 6 whole cloves

2 C. water

1 (16 oz.) bottle barbecue
sauce

Hamburger buns

Place half of the sliced onions across bottom of slow cooker. Set pork roast or picnic ham over onions and top with whole cloves and water. Place remaining sliced onions over top of meat.

Cover and cook on low setting for 10 to 12 hours. Remove meat from slow cooker, drain and remove bone from meat. Shred meat and return shredded meat to slow cooker. Add chopped onions and barbecue sauce. Mix to combine, cover and cook for an additional 30 minutes, or until mixture is heated throughout.

To serve, spoon barbequed pork onto hamburger buns.

Sweet & Sour Spareribs

Prep Time: 20 minutes

Cook Time: 10-12 hours

Servings: 8-10

Ingredients:

1 C. brown sugar

¼ C. flour

⅓ C. water

½ C. vinegar

2 T. soy sauce

¼ C. ketchup

½ tsp. ground ginger

¼ tsp. garlic powder

1 tsp. salt

⅛ tsp. pepper

3 lbs. pork spareribs, cut into 2 to 3 rib sections

In a medium saucepan over medium heat, combine brown sugar and flour. Add water, vinegar, soy sauce, ketchup, ground ginger, garlic powder, salt and pepper. Heat, stirring frequently, until mixture begins to boil. Let boil for 2 to 3 minutes, until thickened.

Layer pork rib sections in slow cooker and spoon sauce mixture over ribs. Cover and cook on low setting for 10 to 12 hours, until ribs are very tender.

To serve, remove ribs from slow cooker using long tongs. Place ribs on a serving platter and spoon remaining sauce mixture over ribs.

Rolled Stuffed Pork Loin

Prep Time: 25 minutes

Cook Time: 10-11 hours

Servings: 6-8

Ingredients:

1½ C. dried breadcrumbs

1 tomato, coarsely chopped

1 (3 lb.) pork loin roast

1 small onion, diced

1 clove garlic, minced

½ C. chopped, cooked bacon

1 tsp. parsley flakes

¼ tsp. dried thyme

¾ tsp. dried basil

2 C. marinara sauce

In a bowl, combine breadcrumbs and chopped tomato, until mixture is moistened and set aside.

Slice pork loin lengthwise along the center, being careful not to cut entirely through. Open the loin like a book and, using a meat tenderizer, pound each side of the loin gently to create a flatter surface, being careful not to pound the sides too thin.

Add diced onion, minced garlic, chopped prepared bacon, parsley flakes, thyme and basil to the breadcrumb mixture. Toss until well combined, adding a tablespoon of water or chicken broth if mixture is too dry. Spoon mixture over pork loin and fold up sides around the stuffing. Tie lengths of kitchen string around pork loin to enclose the stuffing mixture.

Place pork loin in slow cooker. Pour marinara sauce over all. Cover and cook on low setting for 10 to 11 hours. To serve, remove loin from slow cooker. Let cool slightly before removing kitchen string and slicing. Spoon remaining marinara sauce from slow cooker over slices.

Glazed Apple Pork Roast

Prep Time: 10-15 minutes

Cook Time: 10-12 hours

Servings: 8-10

Ingredients:

1 (4 lb.) pork loin roast

Salt and pepper to taste

6 apples, cored and quartered

⅓ C. apple juice

3 T. brown sugar

1 tsp. ground ginger

Trim excess fat from pork roast. Season roast with salt and pepper to taste. Brown pork roast under broiler for 2 to 3 minutes and drain well.

Place quartered apples across bottom of slow cooker. Set pork loin roast over apples.

In a medium bowl, combine apple juice, brown sugar and ground ginger. Mix well and drizzle over roast in slow cooker. Cover and cook on low setting for 10 to 12 hours.

To serve, remove roast and apples from slow cooker and set on a serving platter. Let cool slightly before slicing the roast.

Thai Pork & Rice

Prep Time: 10-15 minutes

Cook Time: 10-12 hours

Servings: 8-10

Ingredients:

2 red bell peppers, seeded

1 (3 lb.) pork shoulder roast

2 tsp. minced garlic

⅓ C. teriyaki sauce

3 T. rice wine vinegar

½ tsp. red pepper flakes

¼ C. unsalted peanut butter

3 C. long-grain white rice, cooked

1 C. chopped unsalted peanuts

1 bunch green onions, chopped

Cut red bell peppers into long, thin strips. Place pork shoulder roast, red bell pepper strips, minced garlic, teriyaki sauce and rice wine vinegar in slow cooker. Sprinkle red pepper flakes over all.

Cover and cook on low setting for 10 to 12 hours. Remove pork roast from slow cooker and shred meat. Add unsalted peanut butter to remaining liquid in slow cooker. Return shredded pork to slow cooker and mix until evenly coated in sauce mixture.

To serve, divide prepared white rice onto serving plates. Place shredded pork and red peppers in peanut sauce over rice on each plate. Sprinkle chopped peanuts and chopped green onions over each serving.

Pork Chops in Mustard Sauce

Prep Time: 15-20 minutes

Cook Time: 10-12 hours

Servings: 6-8

Ingredients:

2 T. vegetable oil

6 to 8 pork loin chops

1 (10½ oz.) can cream of mushroom soup

¼ C. chicken broth

¼ C. Dijon-style mustard

½ tsp. dried thyme

1 clove garlic, minced

¼ tsp. pepper

2 medium potatoes, thinly sliced

1 onion, thinly sliced

In a large skillet over medium heat, place vegetable oil. Add pork chops to skillet and heat, turning once, until browned on both sides. Drain pork chops and set aside.

Combine cream of mushroom soup, chicken broth, mustard, dried thyme, minced garlic and pepper in slow cooker. Add thin potato and onion slices and mix until well combined. Place browned pork chops over potato mixture in slow cooker.

Cover and cook on low setting for 10 to 12 hours. To serve, remove pork chops to a serving platter. Spoon potato and onion mixture around pork chops. Drizzle any remaining sauce from slow cooker over pork chops.

SOUP
&
STEW

Chili Beef

Prep Time: 10-15 minutes

Cook Time: 10-12 hours

Servings: 8

Ingredients:

1 clove garlic, peeled and coarsely chopped

½ tsp. salt

¼ tsp. pepper

1 T. chili powder

1 T. dry mustard

2 lbs. boneless round steak

1 onion, chopped

1 bell pepper, chopped

1 (16 oz.) can whole tomatoes in juice

1 beef bouillon cube

1 (15 oz.) can kidney beans

In a small bowl, combine chopped garlic, salt, pepper, chili powder and dry mustard. Mix well and rub over boneless steak. Cut seasoned steak into strips or cubes and place in slow cooker. Place chopped onion and bell pepper around meat in slow cooker.

Pour tomatoes in juice over ingredients and add beef bouillon and kidney beans. Mix well. Cover and cook on low setting for 10 to 12 hours. To serve, mix lightly and ladle chili into bowls.

Hearty Beef Stew

Prep Time: 10-15 minutes

Cook Time: 10-12 hours

Servings: 8

Ingredients:

3 to 4 lbs. beef roast

1 carrot, coarsely chopped

3 medium potatoes, coarsely chopped

2 stalks celery, chopped

2 cloves garlic, chopped

1 medium onion, coarsely chopped

1 medium parsnip, peeled and coarsely chopped

3 beef bouillon cubes

2 T. Worcestershire sauce

1 bay leaf

½ tsp. paprika

1 tsp. salt

¼ tsp. pepper

Trim excess fat from beef roast and cut into 1" to 2" cubes. Season roast with salt and pepper to taste. Place beef cubes, chopped carrots, chopped potatoes, chopped celery, chopped garlic, chopped onion and chopped parsnip in slow cooker. Mix all together.

Fill a glass measuring cup or bowl with 2 cups warm water. Add beef bouillon cubes, mixing until bouillon is completely dissolved. Add bouillon mixture, Worcestershire sauce, bay leaf, paprika, salt and pepper to slow cooker. The liquid should nearly, but not completely, cover ingredients in slow cooker. Adjust water level if necessary.

Cover and cook on low setting for 10 to 12 hours. To serve, mix lightly and ladle stew into bowls.

Ham & White Bean Stew

Prep Time: Overnight, plus 10 minutes

Cook Time: 10-12 hours

Servings: 6

Ingredients:

6 C. water

1 lb. Great Northern or other white beans

¾ lb. ham

1 medium white onion, coarsely chopped

2 stalks celery, chopped

1 smoked ham hock

1 T. brown sugar

In a large stockpot filled with 6 cups water, soak white beans overnight.

Cut ham into ½" to 1" cubes. Place cubed ham, chopped onion and chopped celery in slow cooker. Drain beans, discarding the water, and add beans to ingredients in slow cooker. Add ham hock and brown sugar and mix until well combined. Add enough water to cover ingredients by about ½".

Cover and cook on low setting for 10 to 12 hours. To serve, mix lightly and ladle stew into bowls.

Chicken & Ham Stew

Prep Time: 10-15 minutes

Cook Time: 10-12 hours, plus 15 minutes

Servings: 6

Ingredients:

3 lbs. chicken leg quarters

2 C. cooked ham, cut into cubes

1 medium onion, chopped

2 stalks celery, chopped

2 medium potatoes, chopped

1 (10 oz.) pkg. frozen lima beans

1 (10 oz.) pkg. frozen corn

2 qts. water

2 chicken bouillon cubes

Place chicken, ham cubes, chopped onion, chopped celery, chopped potatoes, lima beans and corn in slow cooker. Add water and bouillon cubes. Mix lightly.

Cover and cook on low setting for 10 to 12 hours. During last hour of cooking time, remove chicken pieces from slow cooker. Let cool slightly. Meanwhile, skim excess fat from top of stew. Once chicken has cooled, remove skin and pull meat from the bone. Return chicken meat to slow cooker and heat for an additional 15 to 20 minutes, until chicken is heated throughout.

To serve, mix lightly and ladle stew into bowls. If desired, serve with warm bread or various crackers.

Wild Mushroom Beef Stew

Prep Time: 10-15 minutes

Cook Time: 10-12 hours

Servings: 6-8

Ingredients:

1½ to 2 lbs. beef stew meat

2 T. flour

½ tsp. salt

½ tsp. pepper

1½ C. beef broth

1 tsp. Worcestershire sauce

1 clove garlic, minced

1 bay leaf

1 tsp. paprika

2 shiitake mushrooms, sliced

2 carrots, sliced

2 potatoes, diced

1 white onion, chopped

1 stalk celery, sliced

Trim excess fat from beef stew meat and cut into 1" cubes. Place meat in slow cooker. In a small bowl, combine flour, salt and pepper. Mix well and sprinkle over stew meat, stirring until meat is evenly coated.

Add beef broth, Worcestershire sauce, minced garlic, bay leaf, paprika, sliced shiitake mushrooms, sliced carrots, diced potatoes, chopped onion and sliced celery to slow cooker. Toss lightly until well incorporated.

Cover and cook on low setting for 10 to 12 hours. To serve, mix lightly and ladle stew into bowls.

Beef Minestrone

Prep Time: 10 minutes

Cook Time: 10-12 hours

Servings: 8

Ingredients:

1½ lbs. stewing meat

3 C. water

1 medium onion, diced

4 carrots, diced

1 (14½ oz.) can tomatoes in juice

2 tsp. salt

1 (10 oz.) pkg. frozen mixed vegetables

1 T. dried basil

½ C. dry vermicelli

1 tsp. dried oregano

Grated Parmesan cheese

Cut stewing meat into bite-sized cubes or pieces. Combine meat, water, diced onion and diced carrots in slow cooker. Add tomatoes in juice, salt, frozen mixed vegetables, dried basil, vermicelli and oregano. Mix until well combined.

Cover and cook on low setting for 10 to 12 hours. To serve, mix lightly and ladle stew into bowls. Top individual servings with desired amount of grated Parmesan cheese.

Chili Con Carne

Prep Time: Overnight, plus 10-15 minutes

Cook Time: 10-12 hours

Servings: 6

Ingredients:

6 C. water

1 lb. pinto beans

2 lbs. beef roast

1 T. chili powder

1 onion, peeled and coarsely chopped

2 cloves garlic, minced

1 T. beef bouillon granules

1 (29 oz.) can tomato sauce

1 (6 oz.) can tomato paste

In a large stockpot filled with 6 cups water, soak pinto beans overnight.

Trim excess fat from beef roast and cut into large cubes. In a large bowl, toss together beef cubes and chili powder until well coated. Add chopped onion and minced garlic to beef cubes. Drain beans, discarding the water, and add beans to beef mixture. Toss all together and place in slow cooker.

Add enough water to just cover mixture in slow cooker. Stir in bouillon granules. Cover and cook on low setting for 10 to 12 hours. During last 1 hour of cooking time, stir in tomato sauce and tomato paste. Mix well. To serve, mix lightly and ladle chili into bowls.

Veggie Potato Soup

Prep Time: 15 minutes

Cook Time: 12 hours

Servings: 6-8

Ingredients:

1 lb. ground beef*

2 (15 oz.) cans diced tomatoes, drained

2 carrots, sliced

2 onions, sliced

2 potatoes, diced

1 to 2 cloves garlic, minced

1 (12 oz.) can V-8 vegetable juice

1½ to 2 C. sliced celery

2 beef bouillon cubes

2 to 3 C. various frozen vegetables, such as peas, corn, cauliflower, etc.

In a medium skillet over medium heat, brown ground beef. Drain fat from ground beef. Place browned ground beef, diced tomatoes, sliced carrots, sliced onions and diced potatoes in slow cooker. Add minced garlic, V-8 juice, sliced celery, beef bouillon cubes and various frozen vegetables.

Cover and cook on low setting for 12 hours. To serve, mix lightly and ladle soup into bowls.

*If desired, ground beef can be replaced with 3 cups pre-cooked dried beans or lentils to make a vegetarian soup.

Brunswick Stew

Prep Time: 20 minutes

Cook Time: 10-11 hours, plus 15 minutes

Servings: 6

Ingredients:

1 T. vegetable oil

4 lbs. chicken hind quarters

Salt and pepper to taste

1 large carrot, coarsely chopped

2 stalks celery, chopped

3 C. frozen lima beans

1½ C. smoked ham, cut into ½" cubes

3 cloves garlic, minced

2 bay leaves

1 C. chicken broth

1½ C. fresh or canned tomatoes, peeled and seeded

1 C. tomato puree or canned tomato sauce

1 C. barbeque sauce

3 C. frozen corn

In a medium skillet over medium heat, place vegetable oil. Season chicken with salt and pepper to taste. When oil is hot, lightly brown chicken in skillet, turning to brown all sides.

Place chopped carrots and chopped celery across bottom of slow cooker. Place browned chicken quarters over carrots and celery. Place lima beans and cubed ham over chicken.

In a medium bowl, combine minced garlic, bay leaves, chicken broth, seeded tomatoes, tomato sauce and barbeque sauce. Mix well and pour over ingredients in slow cooker.

Cover and cook on low setting for 10-11 hours. Remove chicken from slow cooker. Increase slow cooker to high setting and add frozen corn. Once chicken has cooled, remove skin and pull meat from the bone. Return chicken meat to slow cooker and heat for an additional 15 to 20 minutes, until chicken and corn are heated throughout.

Steak Soup

Prep Time: 15 minutes

Cook Time: 10-12 hours

Servings: 10-12

Ingredients:

2 lbs. coarsely ground beef

5 C. water

1 large onion, chopped

4 stalks celery, chopped

3 carrots, sliced

2 (14½ oz.) cans diced
   tomatoes in juice

1 (10 oz.) pkg. frozen mixed
   vegetables

5 beef bouillon cubes

½ tsp. pepper

½ C. butter, melted

½ C. flour

2 tsp. salt

In a medium skillet over medium heat, brown ground beef. Drain fat from ground beef. Place browned ground beef, water, chopped onion, chopped celery, sliced carrots, tomatoes in juice, frozen mixed vegetables, beef bouillon and pepper in slow cooker.

Cover and cook on low setting for 10 to 12 hours. During last hour of cooking time, increase slow cooker to high setting. In a small bowl, combine melted butter and flour, stirring until smooth. Pour mixture over ingredients in slow cooker and mix well. Mix in salt.

Continue to heat until soup has thickened, about 30 minutes. To serve, mix lightly and ladle soup into bowls.

Black Bean Chili

Prep Time: 15 minutes

Cook Time: 10-12 hours

Servings: 6

Ingredients:

2 lbs. coarsely ground beef

1 (16 oz.) can red kidney beans, drained

1 (15 oz.) can black beans, rinsed and drained

2 (14½ oz.) cans diced tomatoes

2 medium onions, coarsely chopped

1 green pepper, coarsely chopped

2 cloves garlic, minced

2 to 3 T. chili powder

1 tsp. pepper

2½ tsp. salt

Chopped green onions, optional

Sour cream, optional

Shredded Cheddar cheese, optional

In a medium skillet over medium heat, brown ground beef. Drain fat from ground beef. Place drained kidney beans in slow cooker and top with drained black beans. Add diced tomatoes. Layer chopped onions over tomatoes, followed by chopped green pepper. Sprinkle minced garlic, chili powder, pepper and salt over green pepper. Stir once.

Cover and cook on low setting for 10 to 12 hours. To serve, mix lightly and ladle chili into bowls. If desired, top individual servings with chopped green onions, a dollop of sour cream and shredded Cheddar cheese.

Hearty Irish Stew

Prep Time: 10-15 minutes

Cook Time: 10-12 hours

Servings: 8

Ingredients:

1 ½ lbs. lamb stew meat

1 lb. bratwurst or sweet Italian sausage

4 medium potatoes, coarsely chopped

1 small cabbage, cut into eighths

1 medium onion, coarsely chopped

1 stalk celery, chopped

½ tsp. salt

½ tsp. pepper

1 T. chicken bouillon granules

1 tsp. caraway seeds

1 C. dark beer

2 T. apple cider vinegar

Trim excess fat from lamb stew meat and cut into large cubes. Cut bratwurst or Italian sausage into 1" thick slices. Place cubed lamb meat, sliced sausage, chopped potatoes, cabbage pieces, chopped onion and chopped celery in slow cooker. Mix until evenly distributed.

Sprinkle salt, pepper, chicken bouillon and caraway seeds over ingredients in slow cooker. Pour beer and apple cider vinegar over all. Add enough water to just slightly cover the ingredients in slow cooker.

Cover and cook on low setting for 10 to 12 hours. To serve, mix lightly and ladle stew into bowls. If desired, serve with dark rye bread.

Cheesy Chicken Veggie Soup

Prep Time: 10 minutes

Cook Time: 10-12 hours

Servings: 10-12

Ingredients:

1 (10½ oz.) can chicken broth

4 chicken bouillon cubes

1 qt. water

2 C. diced onions

2 C. diced celery

4 C. diced potatoes

3 C. diced carrots

1 (10 oz.) pkg. frozen whole kernel corn

2 (10¾ oz.) cans cream of chicken soup

½ lb. Velveeta cheese, cubed

Combine chicken broth, chicken bouillon cubes and water in slow cooker. Mix lightly and add diced onions, diced celery, diced potatoes, diced carrots, whole kernel corn and cream of chicken soup. Mix well.

Cover and cook on low setting for 10 to 12 hours, or until vegetables are tender. Add cubed cheese to soup and stir until cheese is completely melted. To serve, ladle soup into bowls.

White Chili

Prep Time: 30 minutes

Cook Time: 10-12 hours

Servings: 8-10

Ingredients:

1 lb. Great Northern beans

1 to 2 T. vegetable oil

2 lbs. boneless, skinless
  chicken breasts, cubed

1 medium onion, chopped

2 (4½ oz.) cans chopped
  green chilies

2 tsp. cumin

½ tsp. salt

1 (14½ oz.) can chicken broth

1 C. water

Place Great Northern beans in a medium saucepan and cover with water. Place saucepan over medium heat and bring to a boil. Reduce heat and let simmer for 20 minutes. Drain beans, discarding the water.

Meanwhile, in a large skillet over medium heat, place vegetable oil. Brown cubed chicken in skillet. Remove chicken from skillet and place in slow cooker. Add drained beans, chopped onion, chopped green chilies, cumin, salt, chicken broth and water to slow cooker. Mix until well combined.

Cover and cook on low setting for 10 to 12 hours. To serve, mix lightly and ladle chili into bowls.

Polish Sauerkraut Soup

Prep Time: 10 minutes

Cook Time: 10-12 hours

Servings: 6-8

Ingredients:

1 to 2 T. vegetable oil

2½ C. chopped chicken

4 C. chicken broth

1 (10¾ oz.) can cream of mushroom soup

1 (16 oz.) can sauerkraut, rinsed and drained

1 (8 oz.) pkg. fresh sliced mushrooms

1 medium potato, cubed

2 medium carrots, peeled and sliced

2 stalks celery, chopped

2 lbs. Polish smoked kielbasa, cubed

2 T. vinegar

2 tsp. dried dillweed

1½ tsp. pepper

In a large skillet over medium heat, place vegetable oil. Brown chopped chicken in skillet. Remove chicken pieces from skillet and place in slow cooker.

Add chicken broth, cream of mushroom soup, drained sauerkraut, sliced mushrooms, cubed potatoes, sliced carrots, chopped celery and cubed smoked kielbasa to slow cooker. Mix well and add vinegar, dillweed and pepper.

Cover and cook on low setting for 10 to 12 hours. If necessary, skim fat from top of soup before ladling into bowls.

Pea Soup with Potatoes

Prep Time: 10 minutes

Cook Time: 12 hours

Servings: 6-8

Ingredients:

1 lb. bulk sausage

6 C. water

2 medium potatoes, diced

1 onion, chopped

½ tsp. dried marjoram or thyme

½ tsp. pepper

2¼ C. dry split peas

In a medium skillet over medium heat, brown bulk sausage. Drain skillet and transfer browned sausage to slow cooker. Add water, diced potatoes, chopped onion, marjoram and pepper.

Wash and sort split peas, removing any stones. Add peas to slow cooker.

Cover and cook on low setting for 12 hours. To serve, mix lightly and ladle soup into bowls.

Turkey Stew

Prep Time: 10 minutes

Cook Time: 10-12 hours

Servings: 8

Ingredients:

2 lbs. skinless turkey thighs

5 large carrots, sliced

2 medium onions, chopped

8 medium potatoes, cubed

4 stalks celery, chopped

3 cloves garlic, minced

1 tsp. salt

¼ tsp. pepper

2 T. Worcestershire sauce

1 (15 oz.) can tomato sauce

2 bay leaves

Place turkey thighs in slow cooker.

In a medium bowl, combine sliced carrots, chopped onions, cubed potatoes, chopped celery, minced garlic, salt, pepper, Worcestershire sauce, tomato sauce and bay leaves. Toss until evenly blended and pour over turkey in slow cooker.

Cover and cook on low setting for 10 to 12 hours. Remove bay leaves before serving. Mix lightly and ladle soup into bowls.

Veggie Split Pea Soup

Prep Time: 5 minutes

Cook Time: 10-12 hours

Servings: 4-6

Ingredients:

2 C. dry split peas

4 C. water

1 stalk celery, chopped

1 C. diced potatoes

1 large carrot, chopped

1 medium onion, chopped

¼ tsp. dried marjoram or thyme

1 bay leaf

½ tsp. salt

1 clove garlic

½ tsp. dried basil

Wash and sort split peas, removing any stones. Place peas, water, chopped celery, diced potatoes, chopped carrot, chopped onion, marjoram, bay leaf, salt, garlic and dried basil in slow cooker.

Cover and cook on low setting for 10 to 12 hours, or until peas are tender. Remove bay leaf and garlic clove before serving. Mix lightly and ladle soup into bowls.

Great Northern Bean Soup

Prep Time: Overnight, plus 15 minutes

Cook Time: 10-12 hours

Servings: 6-8

Ingredients:

1 lb. dry Great Northern beans

6 C. water

1 lb. ham

2 medium onions, chopped

½ C. chopped green pepper

1 C. chopped celery

1 (16 oz.) can diced tomatoes

4 carrots, peeled and chopped

1 (4 oz.) can green chili peppers, drained

1 tsp. garlic powder

1 to 2 qts. water

2 to 3 tsp. salt

Wash and rinse Great Northern beans. In a large stockpot filled with 6 cups water, soak beans overnight.

Meanwhile, dice ham into 1" cubes. Drain beans, discarding the water, and place in slow cooker. Add diced ham, chopped onions, chopped green pepper, chopped celery, diced tomatoes, chopped carrots, drained chili peppers and garlic powder. Add enough water to cover ingredients by at least 2" to 3". Stir in salt to taste.

Cover and cook on low setting for 10 to 12 hours, or until beans are tender. To serve, mix lightly and ladle soup into bowls.

Potato Soup

Prep Time: 10-15 minutes

Cook Time: 10-12 hours

Servings: 8-10

Ingredients:

6 potatoes, peeled and cubed

2 leeks, chopped

2 onions, chopped

1 stalk celery, sliced

4 chicken bouillon cubes*

1 T. parsley flakes

5 C. water*

1 T. salt

Pepper to taste

⅓ C. butter

1 (13 oz.) can evaporated milk

Chopped chives, optional

Combine cubed potatoes, chopped leeks, chopped onions, sliced celery and chicken bouillon cubes in slow cooker. Add dried parsley flakes, water, salt, pepper and butter. Mix until well combined.

Cover and cook on low setting for 10 to 12 hours. During last hour of cooking time, stir in evaporated milk. If desired, mash potatoes with a potato masher before serving. Ladle soup into bowls and, if desired, garnish each serving with a sprinkle of chopped chives.

*Water and chicken bouillon cubes can be replaced with 4 to 5 cups chicken broth.

Three Bean Soup

Prep Time: 5-10 minutes

Cook Time: 11-13 hours

Servings: 10-12

Ingredients:

1 C. dry Great Northern beans

1 C. dry red or pinto beans

1 (15 oz.) can black beans, rinsed and drained

4 C. water

1 (28 oz.) can diced tomatoes in juice

1 medium onion, chopped

4 vegetable bouillon cubes

2 cloves garlic, minced

2 tsp. Italian seasoning

1 (9 oz.) pkg. frozen green beans, thawed

Wash and rinse Great Northern beans and red beans. Combine rinsed Great Northern beans, red beans, black beans, water, diced tomatoes in juice, chopped onion, bouillon cubes, minced garlic and Italian seasoning in slow cooker. Mix until well combined.

Cover and cook on low setting for 11 to 13 hours. During last 2 hours of cooking time, stir in green beans. To serve, mix lightly and ladle soup into bowls.

Beef Stew Bourguignon

Prep Time: 15 minutes

Cook Time: 10-12 hours

Servings: 6

Ingredients:

2 T. vegetable oil

2 lbs. stewing beef, cut into
1" cubes

1 (10¾ oz.) can cream of
mushroom soup

1 tsp. Worcestershire sauce

⅓ C. dry red wine

½ tsp. dried oregano

2 tsp. salt

½ tsp. pepper

½ C. chopped onions

½ C. chopped carrots

1 (4 oz.) can mushroom
pieces, drained

½ C. cold water

¼ C. flour

Prepared noodles,
optional

In a large saucepan over medium heat, heat vegetable oil. Add beef cubes and cook until meat is browned. Place browned meat in slow cooker.

In a medium bowl, combine cream of mushroom soup, Worcestershire sauce, red wine, oregano, salt, pepper, chopped onions, chopped carrots and drained mushrooms. Mix well and pour over meat in slow cooker.

Cover and cook on low setting for 10 to 12 hours. In a small bowl, combine cold water and flour, mixing until a paste forms. Increase slow cooker to high setting and add flour mixture, stirring until mixture is thickened and bubbly. If desired, ladle stew over prepared noodles on serving plates.

Irish Lamb Stew

Prep Time: 10-15 minutes

Cook Time: 10-12 hours

Servings: 8-10

Ingredients:

2 lbs. boneless lean lamb meat

2 tsp. salt

¼ tsp. pepper

2 carrots, cut into 1" slices

2 onions, sliced

4 potatoes, peeled and quartered

¼ C. quick cooking tapioca

3 C. water

1 bay leaf

1 (10 oz.) pkg. frozen peas, thawed

Cut lamb meat into 1½" cubes and season meat with salt and pepper. Place sliced carrots, sliced onions and quartered potatoes across bottom of slow cooker. Sprinkle tapioca over vegetables and place seasoned lamb meat over tapioca. Add water and bay leaf.

Cover and cook on low setting for 10 to 12 hours. During last 30 minutes of cooking time, stir in peas. To serve, mix lightly and ladle stew into bowls.

Lentil Soup

Prep Time: Overnight, plus 5 minutes

Cook Time: 10-12 hours

Servings: 10-12

Ingredients:

4 qts. water, divided

2 (16 oz.) bags lentils

1 env. dry vegetable soup mix

2 (15 oz.) cans stewed tomatoes in juice

1 C. frozen chopped onion

1 tsp. salt

1 tsp. minced garlic

2 T. Worcestershire sauce

In a large stockpot filled with 1 quart water, soak lentils overnight.

Drain lentils, discarding the water, and place lentils in slow cooker. Add vegetable soup mix, stewed tomatoes in juice, chopped onion, salt, minced garlic, Worcestershire sauce and remaining 3 quarts water. Mix until well combined.

Cover and cook on low setting for 10 to 12 hours. To serve, mix lightly and ladle soup into bowls.

Beef & Barley Stew

Prep Time: 10 minutes

Cook Time: 10-12 hours

Servings: 6

Ingredients:

1 lb. boneless beef round steak

2 C. frozen green beans

1 C. sliced carrots

1 onion, chopped

3 cloves garlic, minced

½ C. uncooked pearl barley

1 (4 oz.) can sliced
   mushrooms, drained

1 (12 oz.) jar mushroom gravy

3 C. water

½ tsp. dried thyme

¼ tsp. pepper

Trim excess fat from beef steak and cut meat into 1" cubes.

Combine cubed meat, green beans, sliced carrots, chopped onion, minced garlic, uncooked pearl barley, drained mushrooms, mushroom gravy, water, dried thyme and pepper. Mix until well combined.

Cover and cook on low setting for 10 to 12 hours. To serve, mix lightly and ladle stew into bowls.

French Onion Soup

Prep Time: 10 minutes

Cook Time: 10-12 hours

Servings: 4

Ingredients:

3 onions, sliced

2 T. butter, melted

1 pkg. gravy mix

3 C. water

4 slices French bread

4 slices Swiss cheese

Separate sliced onions into rings. Place onion rings across bottom of slow cooker. Pour butter over onions and mix well. Add gravy mix and water. Mix well.

Cover and cook on low setting for 10 to 12 hours. To prepare, place 1 Swiss cheese slice over each French bread slice. Ladle soup evenly into 4 bowls. Float one bread slice on top of soup in each bowl. Place bowls on a baking sheet and place under broiler for 2 to 3 minutes, until cheese is melted and bubbly.

Carefully remove bowls from oven and let cool slightly before serving.

Pork & Pea Curried Soup

Prep Time: 10 minutes

Cook Time: 10-12 hours

Servings: 6-8

Ingredients:

1½ lbs. boneless pork shoulder roast

1 C. dry yellow or green split peas, rinsed and drained

½ C. finely chopped carrots

½ C. finely chopped celery

½ C. finely chopped onions

1 (49½ oz.) can chicken broth

2 tsp. curry powder

½ tsp. paprika

¼ tsp. ground cumin

¼ tsp. pepper

2 C. fresh spinach, torn

Trim excess fat from pork roast and cut meat into ½" pieces. Completely rinse and drain the split peas.

Combine rinsed split peas, chopped carrots, chopped celery and chopped onions in slow cooker. Mix lightly and add chicken broth, curry powder, paprika, ground cumin and pepper. Add pork pieces and mix until well combined.

Cover and cook on low setting for 10 to 12 hours. To serve, stir in torn spinach and ladle soup into bowls.

Bean and Bacon Soup

Prep Time: 10-15 minutes

Cook Time: 10-12 hours, plus 30 minutes

Servings: 6

Ingredients:

4 slices bacon

1¼ C. dry bean soup mix or various dried beans

1 onion, chopped

3 C. water

1 pkg. taco seasoning mix

2 (14 oz.) cans diced tomatoes in juice

In a medium skillet over medium high heat, cook bacon until crisp. Remove bacon to paper towels to drain. Crumble bacon and place in slow cooker. Add beans, chopped onion, water and taco seasoning mix. Stir until well blended.

Cover and cook on low setting for 10 to 12 hours, or until beans are tender. Add diced tomatoes in juice, cover and cook for an additional 30 to 40 minutes. If desired, beans can be mashed using a potato masher prior to adding tomatoes. To serve, ladle soup into bowls.

Potato Meatball Stew

Prep Time: 5-10 minutes

Cook Time: 10-12 hours

Servings: 4-6

Ingredients:

40 frozen meatballs

6 potatoes, peeled and sliced

1 (16 oz.) bag baby carrots

2 stalks celery, chopped

3 (14 oz.) cans chicken broth

1 T. parsley flakes

⅛ tsp. pepper

1 (12 oz.) can evaporated milk

Combine frozen meatballs, sliced potatoes, baby carrots, chopped celery and chicken broth in slow cooker. Mix well and stir in dried parsley flakes and pepper.

Cover and cook on low setting for 10 to 12 hours. During last hour of cooking time, stir in evaporated milk. To serve, mix lightly and ladle soup into bowls.

MISCELLANEOUS

Red Beans & Rice

Prep Time: 1½ hours

Cook Time: 10-12 hours

Servings: 8

Ingredients:

1 lb. dry red beans

1 medium onion, chopped

1 small green pepper, chopped

2 stalks celery, chopped

3 cloves garlic, minced

2 (14½ oz.) cans beef broth

2 C. water

1 lb. smoked ham, cut into 1" pieces

1 tsp. salt

½ tsp. hot pepper sauce

3 to 4 C. prepared rice

In a large pot over medium heat, place dry red beans. Fill pot with water, to within 2" from top of pot, making sure to fully cover beans with water. Bring mixture to a boil for 10 minutes. Remove from heat. Cover pot with lid and let stand for 1 hour. After 1 hour, drain beans and discard water.

Place soaked beans in slow cooker and add chopped onion, chopped green pepper and chopped celery. Add minced garlic, beef broth, water, ham pieces, salt and hot pepper sauce. Mix until well combined.

Cover and cook on low setting for 10 to 12 hours. To serve, place cooked rice on serving plates and spoon bean mixture over rice. If desired, rice may be stirred into bean mixture while still in slow cooker before spooning onto plates.

Lamb with Balsamic Veggies

Prep Time: 10-15 minutes

Cook Time: 10-12 hours

Servings: 8

Ingredients:

1 tsp. salt

1 tsp. pepper

1 tsp. ground coriander

2 tsp. dried rosemary

1 tsp. dried mint

1 tsp. dried thyme

1 tsp. ground fennel

1 (3 lb.) boneless lamb roast

1 large red onion, cut into eighths

2 medium zucchini, cut into ½" slices

2 yellow squash, cut into ½" slices

2 medium new potatoes, quartered

3 T. balsamic vinegar

In a small bowl, combine salt, pepper, ground coriander, dried rosemary, dried mint, dried thyme and ground fennel. Mix well. Trim lamb roast completely of fat and rub seasoning over all sides of lamb roast.

Place seasoned lamb roast in slow cooker. Add red onion pieces, zucchini slices, squash slices and quartered new potatoes. Drizzle balsamic vinegar over vegetables.

Cover and cook on low setting for 10 to 12 hours. To serve, remove vegetables and lamb from slow cooker and place on a serving platter.

Spiced Veggies & Fruit

Prep Time: 10 minutes

Cook Time: 10-12 hours

Servings: 12-16

Ingredients:

3 large carrots

3 medium onions

2 lbs. sweet potatoes

2 lbs. yams

1 C. dried apple rings, quartered

1½ C. pitted prunes

1 C. dried pears, chopped

1 C. dried apricots, halved

1 C. dried sweet cherries

¾ C. dried sour cherries

1 C. dark brown sugar

2 tsp. cinnamon

2 C. orange juice

2 C. sweet or dry white wine

Peel and chop the carrots and onions. Peel the sweet potatoes and yams and cut into thin slices.

Place peeled and chopped carrots, onions, sweet potato slices, yam slices, quartered apple rings and pitted prunes in slow cooker. Add chopped dried pears, dried apricots, dried sweet cherries and dried sour cherries. Stir until well combined. Sprinkle brown sugar and cinnamon over ingredients. Pour orange juice and wine over all and add enough water to completely cover all ingredients.

Cover and cook on high setting for 10 to 12 hours, or until vegetables are very soft. To serve, spoon vegetables and fruit from slow cooker onto a serving platter. Can be served hot or at room temperature.

Southwestern Enchiladas

Prep Time: 10 minutes

Cook Time: 12 hours, plus 30 minutes

Servings: 18-24

Ingredients:

2 lbs. tri-tip steak, cut into chunks

1 C. water

¼ C. tequila

1 clove garlic, minced

1 Serrano chile, diced

Salt and pepper to taste

5 (7 oz.) cans tomatillo sauce

1½ C. tomato sauce

1 lb. shredded pepper Jack cheese

3 (15 oz.) cans black beans, rinsed and drained

1 (7 oz.) can diced chiles, drained

24 (10") flour tortillas

Combine steak chunks, water, tequila, minced garlic and diced Serrano chile in slow cooker. Season with salt and pepper to taste and mix well. Cover and cook on low setting for 12 hours, or until steak is very tender. Remove steak from slow cooker and shred into pieces.

Preheat oven to 350°. In a medium saucepan over medium heat, combine tomatillo sauce and tomato sauce, stirring constantly, until heated throughout. Add ¼ cup of the shredded pepper Jack cheese. In a separate saucepan over medium heat, cook drained black beans until heated throughout.

Fill each flour tortilla with some of the sauce mixture, black beans, shredded cheese and shredded steak. Add a few diced chiles to each and roll to enclose ingredients. Arrange enchiladas in two 9 x 13" baking dishes. Sprinkle any remaining cheese and diced chiles over enchiladas and pour any remaining sauce over enchiladas. Cover pans with aluminum foil and bake in oven for 15 minutes. Serve immediately.

Lemon Herb Roasted Lamb

Prep Time 10 minutes

Cook Time: 10-12 hours

Servings: 4

Ingredients:

4 large potatoes, cubed

1 tsp. salt

6 cloves garlic, peeled and crushed

Zest of 1 lemon

4 sprigs fresh rosemary, chopped

1 boneless leg of lamb, trimmed and tied

2 T. olive oil

½ C. dry white wine

Place cubed potatoes across bottom of slow cooker. In a medium bowl, combine salt, crushed garlic, lemon zest and fresh chopped rosemary. Mix well and rub mixture over all sides of lamb meat.

In a large frying pan over medium heat, heat olive oil. Add leg of lamb, turning until evenly browned on all sides.

Place browned lamb meat in slow cooker. Pour white wine over lamb. Cover and cook on low setting for 10 to 12 hours. To serve, remove leg of lamb and seasoning from slow cooker and place on a serving platter. Let cool slightly before cutting into slices.

Fresh Herbed Turkey

Prep Time: 10 minutes

Cook Time: 10-12 hours

Servings: 8-10

Ingredients:

2 T. butter, softened

¼ C. fresh minced sage

¼ C. fresh minced tarragon

2 cloves garlic, minced

1 tsp. pepper

½ tsp. salt

1 (4 lb.) turkey breast

1½ T. cornstarch

In a small bowl, combine softened butter, minced sage, minced tarragon, minced garlic, pepper and salt. Mix until well combined. Rub butter mixture over all sides of turkey breast. Place seasoned turkey breast in slow cooker.

Cover and cook on low setting for 10 to 12 hours. Remove turkey breast from slow cooker and place on a platter. Increase slow cooker to high setting and add cornstarch to liquid remaining in slow cooker. Whisk mixture together until a thick, smooth sauce forms. Slice turkey into servings and drizzle sauce over each slice.

Stuffing for a Crowd

Prep Time: 15 minutes

Cook Time: 10-12 hours

Servings: 16

Ingredients:

1 C. butter or margarine

2 C. chopped onions

2 C. chopped celery

¼ C. fresh chopped parsley

1 (12 oz.) pkg. sliced
   mushrooms

12 C. dry cubed bread

1 tsp. poultry seasoning

1½ tsp. dried sage

1 tsp. dried thyme

½ tsp. dried marjoram

1½ tsp. salt

½ tsp. pepper

4½ C. chicken broth

2 eggs, beaten

In a medium skillet over medium heat, melt butter. Stir in chopped onions, chopped celery, chopped parsley and sliced mushrooms and heat, stirring frequently, until sautéed.

Place bread cubes in a large bowl and add sautéed vegetables to bowl. Sprinkle with poultry seasoning, dried sage, dried thyme, dried marjoram, salt and pepper. Add enough chicken broth until mixture is moistened and mix in beaten eggs. Toss all together until well combined. Transfer mixture to slow cooker.

Cover and cook on low setting for 10 to 12 hours. Before serving, mix stuffing ingredients with a long spoon.

Jamaican BBQ Sauce

Prep Time: 15-20 minutes

Cook Time: 10-12 hours

Servings: 4 to 5 cups

Ingredients:

3 (10 oz.) cans chicken broth

2 (12 oz.) bottles dark beer

1 large white onion, chopped

1 large red onion, chopped

2 bunches green onions, chopped

2 T. fresh minced gingerroot

1 (4½ oz.) can chopped green chiles

4 T. tamarind concentrate

⅔ C. molasses

4 T. dark brown sugar

2½ T. ground allspice

4 tsp. pepper

4 tsp. cayenne pepper

2 tsp. cinnamon

2 tsp. nutmeg

1 tsp. dried thyme

3 tsp. salt

3 tsp. turbinado sugar*

2 T. soy sauce

2 T. white wine vinegar

2 large green chile peppers, optional

2 jalapeno peppers, optional

Combine all ingredients in slow cooker, mixing until well combined.

If using green fresh chile peppers and jalapeno peppers, roast and chop the peppers before adding to ingredients. To roast peppers, place peppers over hot grill, turning until browned on all sides, or heat in a greased skillet over medium high heat until browned. Chop peppers, discarding the seeds, and add to slow cooker, mixing well.

Cover and cook on low setting for 10-12 hours, until sauce has reduced and thickened. Use as a topping for grilled chicken or pork or in recipes calling for barbeque sauce.

*Turbinado sugar is a honey-colored, large crystal sugar. If you are unable to find turbinado sugar, additional dark brown sugar can be used as a substitute.

Stuffed Bell Peppers

Prep Time: 15 minutes

Cook Time: 10-12 hours

Servings: 8

Ingredients:

2 lbs. ground beef

1 large onion, chopped

1 C. prepared rice

2 eggs, beaten

½ C. milk

½ C. ketchup

Dash of hot pepper sauce

2 tsp. salt

½ tsp. pepper

8 large bell peppers

In a medium skillet over medium heat, lightly brown the ground beef. In a medium bowl, combine lightly browned ground beef, chopped onion, prepared rice, beaten eggs, milk, ketchup, hot pepper sauce, salt and pepper. Mix until well combined.

Cut the top ½" to 1" off of each bell pepper and scoop out the seeds. It may be necessary to slightly cut the bottom of each bell pepper in order for them to stand up on their own. If it is necessary to cut the bottom, be careful not to cut entirely through the pepper, making sure the bottom is still intact.

Scoop ground beef mixture into each hollowed bell pepper. Place peppers upright in greased slow cooker. Cover and cook on low setting for 10 to 12 hours.

Spaghetti Tomato Sauce

Prep Time: 5 minutes

Cook Time: 10-12 hours, plus 25 minutes

Servings: 6

Ingredients:

1 C. finely chopped onions

2 cloves garlic, minced

1 (28 oz.) can chopped tomatoes in juice

1 (6 oz.) can tomato paste

1 T. sugar

2 tsp. beef bouillon granules

1 tsp. dried oregano

½ tsp. dried basil

1 large bay leaf

Salt and pepper to taste

1 (4 oz.) can sliced mushrooms, drained

2 T. cornstarch

2 T. cold water

In slow cooker, combine chopped onions, minced garlic, tomatoes in juice, tomato paste, sugar, beef bouillon granules, dried oregano, dried basil, bay leaf and salt and pepper to taste.

Cover and cook on low setting for 10 to 12 hours. Remove bay leaf and stir in drained mushrooms. In a small bowl, combine cornstarch and cold water. Mix well and stir into sauce in slow cooker.

Cover and cook on high setting for an additional 25 minutes, or until sauce is thickened and bubbly. Serve over cooked pasta or in recipes calling for tomato sauce.

Big Potluck

Prep Time: 10-15 minutes

Cook Time: 10-12 hours

Servings: 10-15

Ingredients:

1 (2½ to 3 lb.) stewing hen, cut into pieces

½ lb. stewing beef, cubed

½ lb. veal shoulder or roast, cubed

1½ qts. water

½ lb. new potatoes, cubed

½ lb. small onions, halved

1 C. sliced carrots

1 C. chopped celery

1 green pepper, chopped

1 (1 lb.) pkg. frozen lima beans

1 C. fresh or frozen okra

1 C. whole kernel corn

1 (8 oz.) can whole tomatoes in juice

1 (15 oz.) can tomato puree

1 tsp. salt

¼ to ½ tsp. pepper

1 tsp. dry mustard

½ tsp. chili powder

¼ C. fresh chopped parsley

In slow cooker, combine stewing hen pieces, cubed beef, cubed veal, water, cubed new potatoes, halved onions, sliced carrots, chopped celery, chopped green pepper, lima beans, okra, corn, whole tomatoes in juice and tomato puree. Mix until well combined.

Cover and cook on low setting for 10 to 12 hours. During last 1 hour of cooking time, stir in salt, pepper, dry mustard, chili powder and fresh chopped parsley.

To serve, remove chicken pieces from slow cooker and de-bone, if needed. Return boneless chicken pieces to slow cooker and mix well. Remove all ingredients to a serving platter and serve immediately.

Baked Beans

Prep Time: Overnight, plus 1½ hours

Cook Time: 10-12 hours

Servings: 8-10

Ingredients:

6 C. water

1 lb. dried navy beans

1 small onion, chopped

¾ C. ketchup

¾ C. brown sugar

¾ C. water

1 tsp. dry mustard

2 T. dark molasses

1 tsp. salt

In a large stockpot filled with 6 cups water, soak navy beans overnight. After 10 to 12 hours of soaking time, cook beans over medium heat for 1½ hours. Drain beans, discarding the water.

In slow cooker, combine drained soaked navy beans, chopped onion, ketchup, brown sugar, ¾ cup water, dry mustard, dark molasses and salt. Mix until well combined.

Cover and cook on low setting for 10 to 12 hours.

Lamb Shanks

Prep Time: 25 minutes

Cook Time: 10-12 hours

Servings: 4-6

Ingredients:

1½ tsp. salt

½ tsp. pepper

2 tsp. paprika

½ tsp. dried rosemary

½ tsp. dried thyme

6 lamb shanks

2 T. vegetable oil

1 (29 oz.) can whole stewed tomatoes in juice

⅓ C. sherry or sweet wine

1 (12 oz.) pkg. pearl onions

In a medium bowl, combine salt, pepper, paprika, dried chopped rosemary and dried thyme. Mix well and rub mixture over lamb shanks.

In a sauté pan over medium heat, place vegetable oil. Heat oil and add seasoned lamb shanks, cooking and turning until lightly browned on each side.

Place browned lamb shanks in slow cooker and add stewed tomatoes in juice, sherry wine and pearl onions. Cover and cook on low setting for 10 to 12 hours.

To serve, remove lamb shanks from slow cooker and place on a serving platter. Spoon tomato sauce and onions from slow cooker over lamb shanks.

Caramelized Onions

Prep Time: 5 minutes

Cook Time: 12 hours

Servings: 6-8

Ingredients:

6 to 8 large Vidalia or other
sweet onions

4 T. butter or margarine,
melted

1 (10 oz.) can chicken or
vegetable broth

Peel sweet onions, removing
the stems and root ends. Place
onions in slow cooker.

Pour melted butter and
chicken or vegetable broth over
onions. Cover and cook on low
setting for 12 hours.

To serve, remove onions
from slow cooker and break
apart with a fork.

Vegetarian Dinner

Prep Time: 10 minutes

Cook Time: 10-12 hours

Servings: 6-8

Ingredients:

6 potatoes, sliced

1 large onion, sliced

2 carrots, sliced

1 green pepper, sliced

1 zucchini, sliced

1 C. fresh or frozen corn

1 C. fresh or frozen peas

2½ C. tomato sauce

¼ C. soy sauce

1 tsp. dried thyme

1 tsp. dry mustard

1 tsp. dried basil

2 tsp. chili powder

½ tsp. cinnamon

⅛ tsp. sage

2 T. parsley flakes

Layer sliced potatoes across bottom of slow cooker. Place onion slices over potatoes and layer sliced carrots over onions. Top carrots with sliced green pepper and sliced zucchini. Top with corn and peas.

In a medium bowl, combine tomato sauce, soy sauce, dried thyme, dry mustard, dried basil, chili powder, cinnamon, sage and dried parsley flakes. Mix until well combined and pour over vegetables in slow cooker.

Cover and cook on low setting for 10 to 12 hours.

Cabbage Rolls

Prep Time: 20 minutes

Cook Time: 10-12 hours

Servings: 8

Ingredients:

8 to 10 large cabbage leaves

8 C. water

1 lb. ground beef

1 egg, beaten

1 (10¾ oz.) can tomato soup

¼ tsp. pepper

4 T. chopped onions

1 C. prepared rice

In a large roasting pan, place cabbage leaves in an even, flat layer. In a medium pot over medium high heat, bring 8 cups water to a boil. Pour boiling water over cabbage leaves and let stand for 5 minutes.

In a medium bowl, combine ground beef, beaten egg, tomato soup, pepper, chopped onions and prepared rice. Mix until well combined. Drain cabbage leaves and place on a flat surface. Divide ground beef mixture evenly among cabbage leaves, placing mixture in the center of each leaf.

Roll up cabbage leaves, fastening the ends with toothpicks. Place filled and rolled cabbage leaves in slow cooker. Cover and cook on low setting for 10 to 12 hours. These cabbage rolls are excellent if prepared the night before and served on the second or third day.

Scalloped Potatoes

Prep Time: 10-15 minutes

Cook Time: 10-12 hours

Servings: 8

Ingredients:

6 russet potatoes, peeled

1 onion, finely chopped

2 cloves garlic, minced

1 (10 oz.) can cream of onion soup

⅔ C. evaporated milk

¼ tsp. salt

⅛ tsp. pepper

¼ tsp. dried thyme

Cut peeled potatoes into ⅛" thick slices. Layer sliced potatoes, finely chopped onion and minced garlic in slow cooker.

In a large bowl, combine cream of onion soup, evaporated milk, salt, pepper and dried thyme. Mix until well combined and pour over ingredients in slow cooker.

Cover and cook on low setting for 10 to 12 hours, or until potatoes are tender.

Sour Cream Braised Lamb

Prep Time: 15-20 minutes

Cook Time: 10-12 hours

Servings: 4

Ingredients:

¼ C. flour

1 tsp. salt

½ tsp. pepper

¼ tsp. dried thyme

¼ tsp. dried tarragon

2 lbs. lamb shoulder or leg, trimmed of fat

¼ C. butter

⅛ tsp. caraway seeds

2 T. beef broth

1 onion, chopped

2 tsp. lemon juice

2 tsp. white wine

1 C. sour cream

In a medium shallow bowl, combine flour, salt, pepper, dried thyme and tarragon. Cut trimmed lamb meat into 1" cubes. Toss lamb pieces in flour mixture until completely coated.

In a medium sauté pan over medium low heat, melt butter. Add coated lamb pieces to pan and sauté until lightly browned.

Place caraway seeds, beef broth, chopped onion, lemon juice and white wine in slow cooker. Add browned lamb pieces. Cover and cook on low setting for 10 to 12 hours.

During last 15 minutes of cooking time, add sour cream to ingredients in slow cooker and mix well. To serve, spoon mixture onto serving plates or into serving bowls.

Jambalaya

Prep Time: 15 minutes

Cook Time: 10-12 hours

Servings: 8

Ingredients:

2 medium onions

2 stalks celery

1 small green pepper

1 small red pepper

2 C. diced sausage

1 (28 oz.) can whole tomatoes in juice

¼ C. tomato paste

3 cloves garlic, minced

1 tsp. parsley flakes

½ tsp. dried thyme

2 whole cloves

2 T. vegetable oil

1 C. raw long-grain rice

1 lb. fresh or frozen shrimp, shelled and de-veined

Coarsely chop the onions and place in slow cooker. Slice celery and add to onions. Remove seeds from green and red pepper, dice peppers and add to celery and onions. Add diced sausage, whole tomatoes in juice, tomato paste and minced garlic to slow cooker. Stir in dried parsley flakes, dried thyme, whole cloves, vegetable oil and long-grain rice. Toss all together until well combined.

Cover and cook on low setting for 10 to 12 hours. During last hour of cooking time, increase slow cooker to high setting. Stir in cleaned shrimp. Cover and cook until shrimp are tender and turned pink, about 1 hour. To serve, spoon jambalaya mixture into bowls.

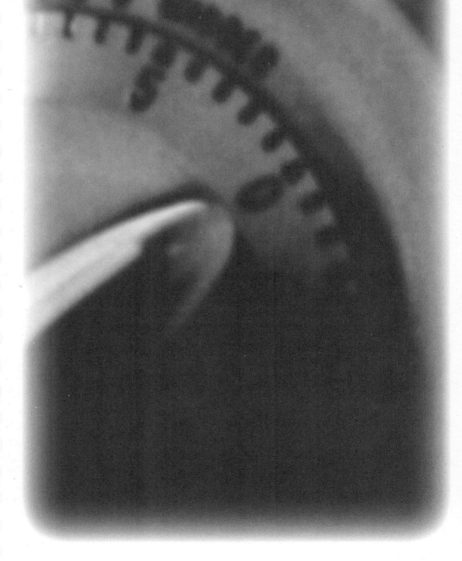

BREAKFAST

Omelet Casserole

Prep Time: 10 minutes

Cook Time: Overnight, or 10-12 hours

Servings: 10

Ingredients:

1 lb. bacon, chopped

1 (32 oz.) bag frozen hash browns, partially thawed

½ C. diced onions

¾ lb. shredded Cheddar cheese

12 eggs

1 C. milk

½ tsp. dry mustard

Salt and pepper to taste

In a medium skillet over medium high heat, cook chopped bacon until crisp. Remove bacon to paper towels to drain.

Layer half of the partially thawed hash browns across bottom of slow cooker. Place half of the cooked chopped bacon in a layer over hash browns. Next, add half of the diced onions followed by half of the shredded Cheddar cheese. Repeat layers in same order, using all remaining hash browns, bacon, onions and cheese.

In a medium bowl, whisk together eggs, milk, dry mustard, salt and pepper. Mix until well combined and pour mixture over ingredients in slow cooker.

Cover and cook on low setting for 10 to 12 hours, or overnight. To serve, use a long spatula to remove omelet casserole from slow cooker.

Breakfast Porridge

Prep Time: 5 minutes

Cook Time: Overnight,
  or 10-12 hours

Servings: 4

Ingredients:

¼ C. cracked wheat

¾ C. old fashioned rolled oats

3 C. water

½ C. raisins

¼ C. wheat germ

½ C. grated apples

¼ tsp. cinnamon

Milk and honey

Combine cracked wheat, old fashioned rolled oats, water, raisins, wheat germ, grated apples and cinnamon in slow cooker. Mix until well combined.

Cover and cook on low setting for 10 to 12 hours, or overnight. To serve, ladle porridge into serving bowls. Serve with a drizzle of milk and honey.

Ham n' Taters

Prep Time: 10 minutes

Cook Time: Overnight, or 10-12 hours

Servings: 6

Ingredients:

1 lb. frozen tater tots

½ lb. cooked ham, diced

½ C. chopped onions

½ C. diced green pepper

¾ C. shredded Cheddar cheese

6 eggs

½ C. milk

Salt and pepper to taste

Layer ⅓ of the frozen tater tots across bottom of slow cooker. Place ⅓ of the cooked diced ham in a layer over tater tots. Next, add ⅓ of the chopped onions followed by ⅓ of the diced green pepper. Top with ⅓ of the shredded Cheddar cheese. Repeat layers two more times in same order, using half of the remaining ingredients each time.

In a medium bowl, beat together eggs and milk using a wire whisk. Add salt and pepper to taste. Mix until well combined and pour mixture over ingredients in slow cooker.

Cover and cook on low setting for 10 to 12 hours, or overnight. To serve, use a long spatula to remove ham n' tater casserole from slow cooker.

Western Omelet

Prep Time: 10 minutes

Cook Time: Overnight, or 10-12 hours

Servings: 12

Ingredients:

1 T. olive oil

1 onion, chopped

1 green bell pepper, chopped

1 (32 oz.) bag frozen hash browns

1 lb. cooked ham, cubed

1½ C. shredded Cheddar cheese

12 eggs

1 C. whole milk

½ tsp. salt

½ tsp. pepper

In a medium skillet over medium heat, place olive oil. Add chopped onion and chopped green pepper. Sauté vegetables until tender but crisp. Remove from heat and let cool for 10 minutes.

Coat inside of slow cooker with nonstick cooking spray. Layer ⅓ of the frozen hash browns across bottom of slow cooker. Add ⅓ of the cubed ham followed by ⅓ of the sautéed onion and green pepper mixture. Top with ⅓ of the shredded Cheddar cheese. Repeat layers two more times in same order, using half of the remaining ingredients each time.

In a large bowl, beat together eggs, whole milk, salt and pepper using a wire whisk. Mix until well combined and pour mixture over ingredients in slow cooker.

Cover and cook on low setting for 10 to 12 hours, or overnight. To serve, use a long spatula to remove western omelet from slow cooker.

Yummy Stuffed Peppers

Prep Time: 15 minutes

Cook Time: Overnight,
or 10-11 hours

Servings: 4-6

Ingredients:

1 lb. breakfast sausage links

4 to 6 large bell peppers

5 eggs, hard boiled

1 tsp. Worcestershire sauce

½ C. chopped onions

½ C. diced tomatoes

2 C. prepared wild rice

1 tsp. dried basil

1 (14 oz.) can diced tomatoes
in juice

1 C. shredded Cheddar cheese

In a skillet over medium heat, cook breakfast sausage links until heated throughout. Remove links from skillet and slice. Meanwhile, slice the top ½" to 1" off of each bell pepper and scoop out the seeds. Peel hard boiled eggs and chop coarsely.

In a bowl, combine sausage slices, chopped hard boiled eggs, Worcestershire sauce, chopped onions, ½ cup diced tomatoes, prepared wild rice and dried basil. Mix until well combined and divide mixture into hollowed peppers.

Pour diced tomatoes in juice across bottom of slow cooker and arrange stuffed peppers, right sight up, in slow cooker, making sure the peppers won't tip over.

Cover and cook on low setting for 10 to 12 hours, or overnight. During last 15 minutes of cooking time, increase slow cooker to high setting and sprinkle each pepper with an even amount of shredded Cheddar cheese. Cover and cook for 15 minutes, or until cheese is melted.

Ham & Apple Breakfast

Prep Time: 5-10 minutes

Cook Time: Overnight,
  or 10-12 hours

Servings: 10-12

Ingredients:

1 (4 to 5 lb.) ham

5 Granny Smith apples, peeled
  and sliced

4 T. butter, melted

½ C. brown sugar

2 tsp. dry mustard

Place ham in center of slow cooker. Arrange sliced apples evenly around ham.

In a small bowl, combine melted butter, brown sugar and dry mustard. Mix until well blended and drizzle over ham and apples in slow cooker.

Cover and cook on low setting for 10 to 12 hours, or overnight. To serve, remove ham to a serving platter. Using a slotted spoon, remove apples and arrange around ham on platter. Let ham cool slightly before slicing.

Hearty Breakfast Hash

Prep Time: 15 minutes

Cook Time: Overnight, or 10-12 hours

Servings: 6-8

Ingredients:

4 C. ground breakfast sausage

¼ C. bacon, diced

6 C. diced red potatoes

1 small onion, finely chopped

1 small bell pepper, finely chopped

1 C. chicken broth

3 T. butter, melted

1 to 1½ C. shredded Cheddar cheese

In a large skillet over medium high heat, combine ground breakfast sausage and diced bacon. Cook, stirring occasionally, until meat is cooked throughout. Drain fat from skillet.

In a large bowl, combine cooked meat, diced red potatoes, finely chopped onion and finely chopped bell pepper. In a small bowl, combine chicken broth and melted butter. Mix well and pour over meat mixture. Toss until well combined and transfer mixture to slow cooker.

Cover and cook on low setting for 10 to 12 hours. During last 10 to 15 minutes of cooking time, increase slow cooker to high setting and sprinkle shredded Cheddar cheese over ingredients. Cover and cook for 10 to 15 minutes, or until cheese is completely melted.

Sausage & Potatoes

Prep Time: 10-15 minutes

Cook Time: Overnight, or 10-12 hours

Servings: 8-10

Ingredients:

1 T. butter

1 lb. sweet Italian sausage links, cut into ½" pieces

1 small onion, diced

3 lbs. Yukon gold potatoes, diced

3 T. maple syrup

Salt and pepper to taste

Scrambled eggs, optional

In a medium skillet over medium heat, melt butter. Add sausage pieces and sauté until sausage is partially cooked. Drain fat from skillet and place sausage in slow cooker.

Add diced onion and diced potatoes to slow cooker and mix with sausage until well combined. Drizzle maple syrup over ingredients in slow cooker and sprinkle with salt and pepper to taste.

Cover and cook on low setting for 10 to 12 hours, or overnight. If desired, serve casserole with scrambled eggs.

Sweet Breakfast Patties

Prep Time: 10-15 minutes

Cook Time: Overnight, or 10 to 12 hours

Servings: 6-8

Ingredients:

½ C. old fashioned rolled oats

½ C. milk

1 lb. chicken breast, finely diced

1 Granny Smith apple, peeled and diced

1 small onion, diced

1 lb. ground breakfast sausage

½ tsp. salt

¼ tsp. pepper

1 tsp. dried sage

¼ tsp. dried thyme

¼ tsp. cinnamon

⅛ tsp. ground ginger

2 eggs, lightly beaten

In a medium bowl, combine old fashioned oats and milk. Set aside and let soak while dicing the chicken, apple and onion.

Add diced chicken, diced apple, diced onion and breakfast sausage to oat mixture in bowl. Add salt, pepper, dried sage, dried thyme, cinnamon, ground ginger and eggs. Knead by hand until well combined.

Place mixture in a greased loaf pan or other heat-safe dish that will fit inside the slow cooker. Set loaf pan in slow cooker. Cover and cook on low setting for 10 to 12 hours, or overnight. Use a hot pad to carefully remove loaf pan from slow cooker. Pour excess fat from top of loaf before turning out onto a serving platter. Allow loaf to cool slightly before slicing into individual patties.

Coffee Cake

Prep Time: 10-15 minutes

Cook Time: Overnight, or 9-10 hours

Servings: 6-8

Ingredients:

2 C. sugar

1 C. vegetable oil

2 eggs

2 tsp. vanilla

2⅓ C. flour, divided

1½ tsp. salt, divided

1 tsp. baking soda

¼ tsp. nutmeg

¾ tsp. plus ½ tsp. cinnamon, divided

2 medium tart apples, peeled and diced

1 C. chopped walnuts

⅓ C. finely chopped pecans

⅓ C. brown sugar

3 T. butter, melted

In a bowl, beat sugar, vegetable oil, eggs and vanilla with a wire whisk until well combined. In a separate bowl, combine 2 cups flour, 1 teaspoon salt, baking soda, nutmeg and ¾ teaspoon cinnamon. Mix well and stir dry ingredients into egg mixture. Fold diced apples and chopped walnuts into mixture. Pour batter into a greased 8 cup loaf pan or other heat-safe dish that will fit inside slow cooker.

Place a metal rack or crumpled foil in bottom of slow cooker. Set filled loaf pan on rack or foil to prevent loaf pan from having contact with the slow cooker.

Cover and cook on low setting for 9 to 10 hours, or overnight. Meanwhile, in a separate bowl, combine remaining ⅓ cup flour, pecans, brown sugar, melted butter, remaining ½ teaspoon cinnamon and remaining ½ teaspoon salt. Mix with a fork until form. Sprinkle mixture over cake during final 30 minutes of cooking time. Use a hot pad to carefully remove loaf pan from slow cooker.

Indian Pudding

Prep Time: 10 minutes

Cook Time: 9-10 hours or overnight,

Servings: 10

Ingredients:

4 C. whole milk, divided

⅓ C. plus 1 T. corn meal

½ C. molasses

4 T. butter

2 T. sugar, honey or maple syrup

1 tsp. ground ginger

¾ tsp. salt

Vanilla yogurt, optional

In a medium saucepan over medium heat, place 3½ cups whole milk. Bring milk just to boiling. Meanwhile, in a small bowl, whisk together remaining ½ cup whole milk and cornmeal. Add cornmeal mixture to milk in saucepan. Continue to cook, stirring constantly, for 3 minutes.

Remove from heat and stir in molasses, butter, sugar, ground ginger and salt. Pour mixture into a greased 8 cup loaf pan or other heat-safe dish that will fit inside the slow cooker.

Place a metal rack or crumpled aluminum foil in bottom of slow cooker. Set filled loaf pan on rack or aluminum foil, preventing the loaf pan from having direct contact with the slow cooker.

Cover and cook on low setting for 10 to 12 hours, or overnight. Use a hot pad to carefully remove loaf pan from slow cooker. If desired, serve pudding with vanilla yogurt.

Wild Rice & Potatoes

Prep Time: 15-20 minutes

Cook Time: Overnight, or 10 to 12 hours

Servings: 8-10

Ingredients:

1 lb. breakfast sausage links

1½ C. prepared wild rice

1 small onion, diced

2 stalks celery, chopped

1½ C. shredded potatoes or hash browns

1 C. chopped bell pepper

½ tsp. salt

¼ tsp. pepper

3 T. butter, melted

1 (10 oz.) can cream of mushroom soup

1 C. chicken broth

1½ C. shredded Cheddar cheese

In a medium skillet over medium heat, place sausage links. Heat links until cooked throughout, remove from skillet and cut into small pieces.

In a large bowl, combine sausage pieces, prepared wild rice, diced onion, chopped celery, shredded potatoes, chopped bell pepper, salt and pepper. In a separate bowl, whisk together melted butter, cream of mushroom soup and chicken broth. Mix well and add to sausage mixture. Toss all together until evenly incorporated.

Transfer mixture to slow cooker. Cover and cook on low setting for 10 to 12 hours, or overnight. During last 10 minutes of cooking time, increase slow cooker to high setting and sprinkle shredded Cheddar cheese over mixture. Cover and cook for 10 minutes, or until cheese is completely melted.

Cranberry Oatmeal

Prep Time: 5 minutes

Cook Time: Overnight, or 10-11 hours

Servings: 2-4

Ingredients:

1 C. old fashioned rolled oats

1 C. dried cranberries

1 C. dried figs

4 C. water

½ C. half n' half

Place old fashioned rolled oats, dried cranberries, dried figs, water and half n' half in slow cooker. Mix until well combined.

Cover and cook on low setting for 10 to 11 hours. Before serving, mix oatmeal with a long spoon and ladle into bowls.

Index

Index

Pork

Soup & Stew

Index

Index

Breakfast